Praises for

WHEN SHE LEADS

Until now, there has been no resource available that spoke directly to women in leadership to prepare them for the task at hand. When She Leads is a crucial read for those considering a career in academia as well as those who have assumed the role for clarity and mentorship.

– Pam Algore,
Retired Principal, 30 years

When She Leads serves as a catalyst for crucial conversations about the future of education for administrators. Information presented in this way is meaningful for the continued sustainability of professionals in this realm.

– JoAnn Jenkins,
School Guidance Counselor, 40 years

As a teacher, this book has given me so much insight about what school administrators are facing and ways in which I can further support the infrastructure of the entire school. This book is not just for administrators but all school professionals and shareholders who have a vested interest in the cultivation of youth.

– Janet Thomas,
Early Childhood Educator, 5 Years

WHEN *She* LEADS

KATRINA RILEY

WWW.13THANDJOAN.COM

When She Leads
Katrina Riley
13th & Joan Publishing

When She Leads. Copyright 2018 by Katrina Riley. All rights reserved. No part of this publication may be reproduced, distributed, or transmitted in any form or by any means, including photocopying, recording, or other electronic or mechanical methods, without the prior written permission of the publisher, except in the case of brief quotations embodied in critical reviews and certain other noncommercial uses permitted by copyright law. For permission requests, write to the publisher, addressed "Attention: Permissions Coordinator," 500 N. Michigan Avenue, Suite #600, Chicago, IL 60611.

13th & Joan books may be purchased for educational, business or sales promotional use. For information, please email the Sales Department at sales@13thandjoan.com.

Printed in the U. S. A.

First Printing, January 2019

Library of Congress Cataloging-in-Publication Data has been applied for.

ISBN: 978-1-733514-6-7

DEDICATION

This book is dedicated to my mother, Corine Riley, who raised me to be a leader and not a follower. Thank you for nurturing me to be great.

EPIGRAPH

What a privilege we, as women, have to be leading during this season in time. It is indeed the year of the woman. It is our time, and we have been given a gift to serve as leaders to build great schools, change lives and communities, and cultivate future, female leaders. Let's create our legacy.

Empowered women possess the capacity to build great schools, cultivate great leaders, impart dynamic change in communities and create a legacy of dreamers, thinkers and doers.

PREFACE

The most powerful world changers are those who resolve to impart knowledge into the hearts and minds of others.

– Katrina Riley

BORN WITH PURPOSE

When I was seven years old, I gave my first public speech in my hometown baptist church in front of a hundred people. One of the things that I talked about during that speech was what I wanted to be when I grew up. I enjoyed playing school, while being the teacher and pretending to teach my teddy bears. I even ventured out to teach my younger brothers and the children that I volunteered with at my mom's daycare center. In the years that followed, people would remind me of that speech about wanting to be a teacher. The elderly ladies at my church would greet me by saying "Oh there is our little teacher."

As the years passed, I matriculated through school with the notion that I would one day become a teacher. I was involved in several school and community based activities and wanted to serve in leadership capacities in all of them. If I couldn't be the president, I had to at least serve on the leadership team. My desire to have the top positions, caused me to question if serving in the capacity of teacher was prestigious? Growing up watching the Cosby Show, whose main characters were a husband and wife whose professions were that of a doctor and a lawyer, also played into that idea. During my high school years, I resolved that I too would become a lawyer. After entering college law school was at the top of my list. While in college, I spent time volunteering in a small, rural school district in Gadsden County, Florida. There was a huge transient, migrant population present.

It felt so rewarding to help students who were struggling to read and to perform on grade level.

Those moments felt right with my soul. By the time I reached my senior year of college, I stopped counting the number of hours that I volunteered with the students. Being in their presence and knowing that my work was impactful realigned me with my original purpose in the realm of education. I made the decision that I wasn't going to be attending law school right away. Instead, I would teach for a few years. Teaching was supposed to be my *gap* year before graduate school.

I felt at home in the classroom. Education had always been and continued to be a natural fit for me. I loved building the connections with students and seeing them grow as learners. Being in the classroom, allowed me to feel confident and secure in my ability to make a difference. I quickly realized that even though I didn't enter the field of education with the intention to stay, this was where I belonged.

KATRINA RILEY

A TRUE LEADER THIRSTS FOR MORE

Even though I was where I belonged, something inside of me longed to be and do more. I wanted to be impactful in the lives of many more students. The facts remained that I loved teaching and I loved my school, but deep down, I felt that I could be a better administrator. I also felt that the school that I was in could improve with the right leadership. I must admit that growing up, I didn't know that being a principal was a possibility or that it could be my reality. It wasn't even a thought of mine when I began teaching. All of my experiences with people in the principalships were male and white. In my mind, I did not meet the demographic. I had always been so ambitious but becoming a principal seemed like it was not attainable for me. This same pattern of thought is what made me resolve to work hard to beat the odds when I made up my mind that a career in educational leadership was what I was after.

Prior to becoming a principal, I landed a phenomenal coaching job with a top educational non- profit, where I was tasked to coach principals and their leadership teams. I've went on to hold a government job coaching principals on how to improve their leadership practices. Each of those roles prepared me for greater. Although these opportunities afforded me great insight into the profession, my heart and my mind was set on becoming a school principal. I knew that I needed to be in charge of student achievement. Driven with determination, I would eventually realize my dream. In doing so, I learned that aspiring to a role and serving in it are two completely different things. As a principal, I learned more than I had ever learned because the ball was in my court.

I found out that when you observe the role from afar, you think you know as much or more than the principal, but nothing compares to true engagement and responsibility in the role. I witnessed extremely high rates of turnover in leadership due to a multitude of factors. I witnessed

many professionals who began the journey to the principal's seat but left the position for various reasons, including burnout and lack of support. I can also remember being judgmental of those who didn't last in the role. I watched so many hard working principals be removed or demoted from their positions with less than five years of experience. I didn't know why, and it scared me. I would later come to recognize that there was something that people who had held these roles before us had failed to tell us.

I wondered on so many occasions how these scenarios could be avoided? Where was the training to keep administrators encouraged? Where was the support that demonstrated what leaders in the role of education should look like? What mistakes had I already made and what factors would play a role in my downfall if not addressed?

SELF-PRESERVATION MUST NOT BE OPTIONAL

My career would eventually allow me to realize the role of principal at two schools in two different states. I know without question that I've been many things to many people while serving in those positions. Even so, making the decision to exit the positions both times was difficult. At the time, I felt that my leaving was premature. In this age of school accountability, school results must be quick and drastic. When I was a principal, there were times when I felt I was drowning, as so many administrators do. I spent long, sleepless hours crafting and revising plans, and gathering resources to make changes in the buildings I was blessed to be leading. I missed family gatherings, put my personal needs aside and made the schools a priority in my life. When you give so much of yourself to a system that you believe in, it is hard to walk away. In life there are times when walking away is what is best for you and you must choose yourself at all costs for your continued sustainability.

Just before the start of my last school year as a principal, a shift happened. It was painful and I felt defeated, but I knew that the shift was necessary. I was gifted with a disappointment that was indescribable. I found myself in a place experiencing those same feelings from my childhood when I felt the urge to fight the calling to be a teacher. Those thoughts would force me to battle with myself to stay in a field that I had loved for my entire life. I had worked so hard to establish myself as a leader but the reality was that I had an epiphany that what I really loved was the element of coaching. It was now clear to me that serving in a capacity to empower others through inspirational techniques and methodologies was what my heart sought to do.

I came to the realization that I was not going to be able to effectively perform these tasks in my role as principal. After observing for so many years, I knew that I wasn't alone and therefore I developed the courage to create a vision for what I knew that others like me needed. I began to develop theories and to collect information that would serve as resources to support those on the front lines, school principals. This book is a result of the courage to coach, the courage to mentor and the courage to provide valuable insight to other educators- especially female educators.

ACKNOWLEDGEMENTS

*W*RITING A BOOK has always been something that I have wanted to do, but I just never thought it would become a reality. Throughout my life, I have learned so many things about leadership. I have been surrounded by people who have instilled the importance of leadership in my life, and I am grateful. Writing this book has served as a platform for the expression of the experiences I have had as a leader in education. I felt that my experiences would help others in their journey to become leaders.

For me, penning this book has been a journey of its own.

I would like to thank some people who have been a part of this wonderful journey with me:

MY FAMILY

My mother, Corine Riley, has always encouraged me to be a leader, and she continues to encourage me during this writing process, even when I wasn't sure what I was doing. I thank you for pushing me to be great and for setting the foundation for my life. You have been my number one supporter, and I thank you for raising me to be strong and independent. You and daddy did a great job!

My brothers Dewayne, Terry, Marty and Ira who liked, shared and followed me on social media during this process. I'm the only girl, and this was a great way to "spoil" me.

My sweetheart, Lydell Sapp who allows me to be who I am without apology. I thank you for supporting me through this process and over the past two years. You didn't complain when I took a leave from my job and decided to start a business and write this book. You gave me the space I needed to get things done and supported me during every step of this process. I truly love and appreciate you.

MY FRIENDS

My ride or die, super friends who have become sisters. You check on me every day. You are my number one fans. You tell me the truth even when I don't want to hear it. During this process, you cheered me along and were the first to hear my drafts and buy my products. Thanks for every like, share, and mention during this process. I love you all beyond words. A special thanks to my bestie Lakesha Mack, my cheerleader, N'Deeo Hicks, and my girlfriend getaway gang—Natonia Davis, Melody Fredrick, and Julie Mouton, and my "what if" crew Angel Johnson and Andytra Lewis.

Leadership isn't just about the individual leader but about those she leads, her leaders and her team. I would like to thank those people who have allowed me to lead them and offer words of advice, often times unsolicited. I'm thankful for the heart to lead as well as those that were open to my leadership and those that followed me and believed in my vision. Both opportunities helped shape me as a leader, and I will always be grateful. I learned the greatest lessons about leadership and myself with my George Washington Carver Team. I was able to lead differently and from a space of caring because of your acceptance of me. You were not the only team that I led, but you were by far my favorite.

I wish to thank the ladies whose leadership I had the opportunity to witness as they led me and others while I was developing my own leadership style and identity. A special thanks to my mentor, Iranetta Wright, who took a chance on me when I was a young middle school English teacher and new to the city. You gave me the opportunity to learn from you, and you let me "pick" your brain for hours whenever I needed something. You taught me how to bring passion to my work for kids. You are the best at what you do! You are a great balance of tough love and support and have been on team Riley from the beginning. Thanks for believing in me and pouring into my life- I have learned the WRIGHT way.

When She Leads
BOOK PROJECT ACKNOWLEDGMENTS...

I WANT TO THANK my dear classmate, Ardre Orie and her team at 13th & Joan Publishing. I am so proud of your work as a publishing company and as a female owned business. You inspired me to take action towards my dreams, and I am so thankful for your support and coaching during this writing journey. You are a solid professional, and this couldn't have been a better partnering to pay homage to our roots. Good things come from good ole' Gainesville, Fl.

I am so thankful to the ladies who contributed to my book as featured authors. Thanks for the candor in your responses and the willingness to share your experiences with others. Your insight will inspire other female leaders for years to come. I can't wait to see what the future holds.

When I started this process, I wanted to work with females with whom I could connect deeply with. What better way to build a lasting legacy than to partner with a former student. Special thanks to Ryoanne Childs, owner of Ryoanne Nichole Photography, who captured the images for my book cover. You are extremely talented and have always been a sweet spirit. I pray that God will continue to bless you and your business.

Additional thanks to the two ladies who made me look fabulous for my cover shoot- Hair designed by Lisa Virgo and Make Up by Myra Drayton-Makeup Artist and Skin Care Specialist.

INTRODUCTION

While growing up, I never had a female principal. At that time, I hadn't given it much thought. Somehow, I ended up in the classroom, as a teacher, with a huge desire to run a school. I found many books written on school leadership; however, few existed that were dedicated to the female principal and the specific challenges we face. The words in this book are the words of advice I wish I would have had as a new principal.

This book will give you helpful information on balancing your life as a female principal. When She Leads is a real discussion on what female school leaders encounter, and it presents some strategies on how to avoid some of the challenges that we encounter while balancing leadership and life. In 2014, 27% of the principals were leaving the principalship due to many factors, including stress, poor preparation and a lack of support. When She Leads is written to help female principals garner the skills needed to reduce stress. It provides a real voice of support to decrease the number of principal turnovers. I know, first hand, what it is like balancing the principalship and life. I have over a decade of school leadership experience. I have worked as a school principal, leadership coach and a professional practice improvement specialist for leaders.

As the author of this book, I desire to bring you a different message about school leadership. This book will give you a real voice of support to help you navigate the beginnings of your principalship role as a woman! It is written for a woman by a woman and designed with you in mind; it is not your typical textbook on school leadership. When She Leads, designed to inspire and encourage, offers proven practical practices for success in leadership. It is void of out of touch research and tons of charts and graphs. Instead, here is a leadership book with real world examples and stories on how to survive in a demanding career as a female school leader. It is a quick and easy read to give you the tools to implement immediate systems of support for you, as the school leader.

Each chapter lifts the curtain to reveal real world scenes of the principalship, and you will find examples through a recall story of what it's really like being a female principal. "How to" steps are explained with a detailed voice and dose of realness. Each chapter has takeaway tips and thought provoking workbook style questions to spark action for the reader. Listen to the voices of some extraordinary women in leadership as they speak from the heart on leadership practices, beliefs, perceptions and the positive impact of mentorship.

Table of Contents

PREFACE IX
ACKNOWLEDGEMENTS XV
BOOK PROJECT ACKNOWLEDGEMENTS XIX
INTRODUCTION XXI

CHAPTER 1:
No One will Bring You Lunch: The Difference Between Male and Female Leaders 1

CHAPTER 2:
Avoiding Burnout 19

CHAPTER 3:
The Different Faces of Female Leadership 31

CHAPTER 4:
Girl Power- Managing Men 49

CHAPTER 5:
Finding the Right Fit: Accepting the Right Position and Why it Matters Most to Women 59

CHAPTER 6:
Girl Code- Taking Care of Other Women in Leadership 81

Chapter 7:
Own Your Feelings 89

Chapter 8:
Supergirl- Effective Delegation for Getting it All Done 101

Chapter 9:
Top Mistakes Female Principals Make and How to Avoid Them 113

Chapter 10:
New Principal 101 153

Chapter 11:
Her Story- Case Study #1 Jennifer Brown 159

Chapter 12:
Her Story- Case Study #2 Iranetta Wright 159

Chapter 13:
Her Story- Case Study #3 Sonia Martin 167

Chapter 14:
Her Story- Case Study #4 Krystal Lofton 173

Chapter 15:
Her Story- Case Study #5 Deborah Ward 181

About the Author 187
Connect with Katrina Riley 189

Chapter 1
NO ONE WILL BRING YOU LUNCH:

THE DIFFERENCE BETWEEN MALE AND FEMALE LEADERS.

I REMEMBER WORKING FOR a charismatic, male principal towards the end of my assistant principal career. He was great; people loved him. When he was under pressure, his front office team of ladies would guard his front office as if were fort knox. They brought his favorite candy, fixed a plate for him at staff luncheons and delivered it to his office. They even made occasional lunch runs on the days he was super busy. If he appeared to be stressed, people would close the door for him. These were gestures I noticed while working under male principal leadership. The females seemed to be more supportive of male principals, and they had a nurturing nature towards these men. If he had to work for longer hours, someone would be there to take care of him. I had never seen these same amenities extended to female principals.

When I became a principal, that was not the case. No one would ever close the door for me, as a safeguard. It did not happen for me and my female colleagues.

Regardless of gender, leadership styles vary from person to person. However, the differences come from the prescriptives and expectations that others have for female leaders.

How others respond to females in leadership is the real difference and where the perception of difference among gender stems from.

While preparing for the principalship, I discovered that female leaders' performance actions were different from the male. I have also learned that many people respond differently to female leaders. Fortunately, I have had the opportunity to work with both male and female leaders. There is a clear distinction in the responses of employees to female leaders, the response to female leaders are the exemplars of female leadership differences among men and women. Below are three examples of the different perceptions that people have of female leadership:

MEN AS SINGLE-TASKERS VS WOMEN AS MULTITASKERS

The issue that women are biologically better at performing numerous duties simultaneously is quite debatable. Men, being single-taskers, are allowed to work in silos. This means they have the privilege of shutting themselves in and focusing on one job until it is completed. Women are better at multitasking but are seldom allowed to close a door to get the pending task done without having to subtly ask for permission to do so. How many times have you gone to your staff and said, "I think I'm going to need a few minutes to get this task done, okay?" Though this is a biological fact, it is also a setback to the population of female leaders. This is a mindset that keeps the female's hands full while the male has to deal with one or two issues at a time. Women are expected to do it all and handle it all, all at the same time. At the household level, a woman can perform house chores, watch the baby and work at the same time. This translates to doing countless jobs altogether at the workplace.[1] People fail to notice the pressure imposed on women who work as principals. No matter how effective one is at getting things done, there is the need for space, time and concentration; however, there is little assurance of this need when it comes to women. Women who work as principals often have to work on projects, respond to calls, receive guests and supervise other workers within a limited time schedule. An orientation of this mindset often leads to females being seen as lower performers. Males are perceived differently when performing under a lot of pressure. In many of our daily interactions with others, we reinforce that mindset and men have witnessed this as well and directly or indirectly men replicated that behavior. There is a need to understand that females are humans. Multitasking should not

---

1 Borreli, Lizette. "Why Women's Brains Are Better Than Men's At Multitasking: Brain Power Linked To Age And Gender." *Medical Daily*, 17 Nov. 2016, www.medicaldaily.com/why-womens-brains-are-better-mens-multitasking-brain-power-linked-age-and-404602.

be an excuse to flood them with work they cannot get done in time.[2] Encouraging that mindset will continue to set unrealistic expectations for female principals. It's up to us to change this.

THE GREAT MYTH: MEN ARE IMPERFECT, WOMEN ARE FLAWLESS

Societal expectations reveal that females should be perfect in everything. I believe that society still holds a view of women being perfect, little angels that don't make any mistakes. Women face daily scrutiny on their qualifications and abilities in almost any context. In order to be hired, women must exemplify perfection in job interviews, at work, parenting, in academics and general lifestyle. Female leaders are expected to be almost perfect, and they must be highly knowledgeable and require no additional support for the job. If female leaders are lacking anything, they must learn quickly, on the job, to be successful. A small window of time might be provided or allotted for women, who are in leadership roles, to make any errors or mistakes. One can't imagine what female leaders go through unless you've held the principal's position. Women are being crucified for mistakes similar to Hester Prynne from the Scarlet Letter. If you are considering being a principal or currently working in a principal's position, it's important for you to know that you will undergo serious perusal and

---

2   Merrill, Douglas. "Why Multitasking Doesn't Work." *Forbes*, Forbes Magazine, 26 Sept. 2012, www.forbes.com/sites/douglasmerrill/2012/08/17/why-multitasking-doesnt-work/#174abde76ada.

face criticism. See it as an opportunity to become more adept to the expectations of the job. Your skills will be strengthened, and you will learn to face the challenges that are a part of the profession. It is, however, unfair when females are being sacrificed for making a mistake while men are just scorned for the same. This bias is wrong, and it negatively affects the workforce and motivation of female leadership. As a leader, you should be responsible and provide positive input in the school environment. You won't be perfect, and making mistakes is a part of being human. Female leaders should not face harsher criticism than their male counterparts. Again, this is a bias that is in the mindset of most people. This double standard can cause female leaders to be afraid to ask for help when it is needed because we don't want to appear weak or less than. A defining practice of this caliber can be detrimental to your success and career trajectory. People need to be understanding when women make mistakes, and they should be offered strategies for improvement. Remember, mistakes are the best way to learn one's lesson. One needs to go down so that she can go up; female leaders, perfect or not, are no exception.

THE GREAT MYTH: MEN ARE PASSIONATE, WOMEN ARE IRRATIONAL

An addition to the perception list is the claim that women are emotional, while men are not. How many times have you heard that women lead with emotions? I am sure you have heard that women are too emotional. The last time I checked, it can still be validated that all humans have emotions; women are not void of them. All human beings have emotions. Men are considered level-headed and hence, rational decision makers, while women are perceived as a bundle of emotions, unfit for making the best decisions. This is another wrong and biased assumption that degrades the ability of female leaders in making good and acceptable decisions just because they show more emotions than men do. For instance, when men yell and curse in a workplace, they are referred to as passionate. When women attempt the same behavior, they are referred to as being moody and emotional. Women have been described as being naturally soft and seen as vulnerable and compassionate. These are traits that do not match the societal definition of strong leadership. What people fail to realize is that these characteristics are important in solving problems and building relationships within the workforce and staff management. These are qualities a principal should be able to achieve. Male leaders are seen as heroic and passionate when they incorporate these traits at work; females face disapproval. When a female exhibits passion, she is perceived as being irrational. When a male shows the same, he is seen as being dedicated to his job. This is unfair to female leaders and for the gender to which it comes so naturally. To be able to reach the position of a principal, a female must exhibit traits of excellent decision making and rationality. It would be unethical to rate her as emotional because she is showing passion as a leader, just because of her gender.

FEMALES MUST BE NURTURERS:

So what does this mean for you as a female principal? It means that you have to recognize that there are differences of perception that exist, but you must decide to show up as your true authentic self, a female who can lead just as well as any man. Recognize that no one is going to bring you lunch, so don't take it personally. This does not necessarily mean that your employees do not care about you or look up to you as their leader. It is a perception of the need of a female versus the need of a male. Rather, it is the natural human mindset that implies that women are the ultimate sustainers, and they have the ability and responsibility to take care of everything and everyone. For instance, taking a cup of coffee to your male boss is typical and pleasing. He has been working all day. However, for female leaders, the trend is rarely heard of. She will spend hours in a meeting and still be expected to get her lunch. Employees are not deliberately being rude when they are more nurturing to male leaders; It is a subconscious certainty that, as a female, the leader has self-maintenance installation. Perception is indeed reality. For most people, an accomplished female principal is a manifestation of strength and endurance. She is expected to show these traits no matter the pressure she is under. This sort of additional responsibility outlays another difference between the perception of male and female leaders.

IT'S THE SEASON FOR FEMALE SCHOOL LEADERSHIP:

As schools are needing more support to transform an entire school, as well as a community, principals who possess transformational leadership styles are becoming highly desirable. Quite naturally, based on everything outlined, females should be the natural fit for school principalship because of the natural traits that we possess. Ladies, this is our season; it's our time. Let's show up as our true authentic selves because we have what it takes to propel the next generation of female leaders and change communities.

As various leadership styles are being studied, there has been an increase in the importance of incorporating transformational leadership into the system. According to the article " Who Makes a Better Leader: A Man or a woman?" by Sebastian Bailey, transformational leadership entails role-model influence, inspiration and motivation, innovation and individual consideration. All these aspects, the latter especially, reflect the importance of sensitivity to leadership. This seals the idea that female leaders need to show sensitivity on top of strength to receive respect from her employees. Males usually need their strength display, and respect comes knocking. The characteristics of transformational leadership include;

> READINESS TO EXPERIENCE– This involves emotional and mental openness to view and understand the world in different dimensions. Transformational leadership is about seeing the bigger picture and from different angles while embracing the facts. This will help the leader to make decisions based on the whole story.
>
> INDIVIDUAL INTEREST– A transformational leader has their eyes on their followers. They take an interest in their state, life, and productiv-

ity. As a leader, the performance of your workforce is a reflection of your effort. A leader needs to show genuine concern over the subjects, give them motivation, help them solve problems and provide a conducive environment for production.

CONSCIENTIOUSNESS – This generally describes an organized and vigilant leader. To be responsible for certain duties, one has to have a form of organization. A transformational leader is systematic and careful by nature. Making mistakes, due to a lack of planning or disorganization, are out of the question. This trait is important in ensuring that duties are detail oriented, performed correctly, smartly and in time. A chaotic organization eventually crumbles, and the leader of such has no base for leadership.

CHALLENGING – Pushing workers to their level best is a trait any leader has to possess. A transformational leader seeks to change the ordinary into the extraordinary. This is why it is important to integrate challenges for the workers. It encourages further development, operability, and competitiveness. A workforce with these traits is destined for greatness. The leader can set out contests to encourage increased productivity. Challenging also triggers innovation and creativity.

For female leaders, joining in on the trend of leadership is vital. Transformational leadership is slowly growing in effect, and women need to embrace it to be at the top of the game. It is advantageous for female principals to face higher expectations in order to be prepared to exponentially lead. Women must continue to strive and achieve in order to broaden our effectiveness in leadership to uplift ourselves and others around us.

SYSTEMS FOR FEMALE ADMINISTRATORS

It is important to implement a plan that involves taking care of oneself and others, as well as improving effectiveness. With the knowledge of how people respond to male and female leadership, I have resolved that it is imperative for us to create an effective self-care system for success. To navigate through the role of a female principal, I have put several strategies in place.

SEVEN STRATEGIES FOR A FEMALE LEADERSHIP SYSTEM

DELEGATION

I take cautionary measures against doing everything at once. The fact that females can do many things at once does not mean they should. Being a female can be tough; you have to deal with the home, children, husband, elderly parents, bills and pets. The position of principal sets a different tone. As a principal, you are responsible for the school, buildings, students, teachers, financial structure and the community. The settings in the home and in the school are almost similar; one could align the school to home and students to kids. However, there is a major difference. A school has a bigger to-do list, and it is inaccurate to assume it will be easy to accomplish all of the entities at the same time; therefore, delegating is an essential strategy. School principals must make sure that they delegate to someone they can trust to complete the tasks. When you master delegating, you will find that you, as well as staff members and students with benefit. The principal will have more time, others will be trained in leadership, and students will receive the expertise of other staff members. Acquiring and building capacity among staff members will be extremely important in maximizing potential.

MANAGE YOUR TIME

Making a schedule is one of the secrets to success in any field. Mark important events in your calendar to help you remember. You may use a journal or reminders; you can use whatever method that works best for you. Set time aside for tasks that you think will need time to complete, such as taking rounds in the classrooms. Mark meetings, appointments and projects that need to be done on your calendar. Time managing also helps you be punctual, hence effective. You will not easily forget important dates, and this works well to improve your job performance.

ASKING FOR HELP

Female leaders have a difficult time trying to satisfy people's expectations of perfection. They, therefore, find it hard to ask for help when they are stuck. This may cause a problem because being a principal is not a one-man job. It requires a certain degree of consultancy. However, you need to be careful. Some people are not as trustworthy as they may seem. They may pretend to be your supporters, but they are genuinely unhappy about the elevation of your position. You need to be prudent when choosing your confidante. Once you find someone trustworthy, you should seal the trust by mutual sharing of problems and ideas. This way, the operation will thrive under the support of others. Invest in a principal coach who offers virtual coaching and ongoing support. A coach can help you troubleshoot problems and develop quick solutions. A good resource for principal coaching is www.principalnerd.com

SETTING YOUR LIMITS

As a principal, you have a standard of dignity that should not be lowered. First of all, you need to be resilient. Remember that the school has a code of conduct that everyone must follow. Those who violate it should face the consequences. Being lenient will only give the opportunity for more violations and complete chaos. You should also be assertive. Let your yes and no mean exactly that. Wavering from your decision shows instability, which can enable people to exploit you. Develop a notion of zero tolerance to nonsense, excuses and unnecessary meetings. Setting a standard gives the understanding that you expect excellence and that you represent excellence. As the principal, your demeanor should reflect that you deserve respect.

TIME OPTIMIZATION

This concept is different from managing time since it deals with maximizing time on getting the important tasks completed. As a principal, many groups of people with different interests will call on you. You do not have time for all of them; you need to trim your schedule. Strategic plans must be implemented to optimize time. Involve staff members in the implementation by agreeing on cues, signs and communication. Specifically, you could have someone to call you out of a meeting that is extending beyond recorded time. Have your secretary sort out emails, calls, and messages and discard the unnecessary ones. Saying "no" to appointment attempts by unannounced people like salespeople and politicians can save time. Ensure that serious school matters always receive priorities.

ATTEND THE DOCTOR'S APPOINTMENT

Make sure you keep a schedule of regular medical check-ups and stick to it. Principals have a major responsibility that involves a lot of physical and psychological engagement. Maintaining your health must become a priority. As the self-care part of the system, you need to keep your health in check. The school will be standing when you return.

BE ORGANIZED

Having a system of order is important. It saves time and promotes performance. Invest in file systems, desk organizers and electronic folder systems. This redirects time and energy, and It minimizes the time that is spent looking for misplaced items.organization affords us the opportunity to promote beneficial activities.

SELF-DEVELOPMENT

You need to grow yourself as a leader. Attend conferences to educate you about trends and recent developments in the learning system. Develop social interactions with peers and learn through others. This will help you learn tips on what to avoid and what to do in certain situations. Invest in a membership that offers educational resources for principals so that you can stay current and relevant. Look for memberships that offer resources related to your expertise and demographics with whom you may be working. Many of the memberships offer discounts to their annual conferences and materials. Check out www.principalnerd.com or www.ascd.org.

FINAL TAKEAWAYS OR TIPS

- Being promoted to a principal is a big step, and as always, it comes with great expectations and responsibilities. It is also an indication of your relentless hard work. You should, therefore, enjoy it and perform in it.

- In the workplace, you must take care of yourself first so that you can be effective for the team that you are leading.
- Remember to put yourself first. On days when you feel like you want someone else to take care of you, that person is in the mirror.
- Don't get caught up on the differences between male and female leaders. Use your skills that you possess to be a great leader. It's our season to lead!

TIP:

Identify a trustworthy personal check person. This is the person that is likely a member of the hospitality team and respects the positions, title and hierarchy. This person may be your assistant principal or one of the office staff members. Search out your staff members to find the right fit for you. For me, it was my secretary. She had a very sweet and caring personality, and I could tell she would be the perfect check person for me. I shared that I had a bad habit of not eating and that I needed her to help me take the time to eat lunch. Once you have identified that person, ask her to be your check person. Give her your signs of when you need a break, and your code word to get you out of a meeting that is running long. Sharing signs of when you need help or a break will help you maintain job fitness.

Reflective Questions
FOR READERS

1. Can you describe a time when you neglected to be attentive to your needs due to work?

2. Whom do you have on your staff that can be a great check person? Why?

3. When you close your office door, who blocks for you?

Chapter 2:
AVOIDING BURNOUT

EVERY YEAR, SCHOOLS lose good principals, and the major reasons cited are stress and the demand of the job. Both are unavoidable. No one should expect the work of a principal to be easy. In fact, it is the exact opposite. A good principal spends the eight paid hours doing work that pertains to others , such as classroom observations, cafeteria duty, meetings, conferences and managing daily operations. Many other hours are used to plan for the work, including drafting emails. It is easy to find yourself staying at work late and bringing work home. Principals are working in a new era, the era of accountability and high stakes testing, which makes the job of the principal very demanding. The strong desire to be successful and to impact change tends to drive us to work super hard, and it causes us to not sleep. We miss workouts, neglect spouses and significant others. A school principal, working under these new conditions and expectations, is vulnerable to experience burnout on the job.

WHAT ARE THE SIGNS OF BURNOUT?

The signs of burnout are described as lack of motivation, extreme tiredness, cynical thoughts about work, and a rise in health concerns. David Ballard, PsyD, of the American Psychological Association, describes job burnout as "an extended period of time when someone experiences exhaustion and a lack of interest in things, resulting in a decline in their job "A lot of burnout really has to do with experiencing chronic stress, " says Dr. Ballard, who is the head of the APA's Psychologically Healthy Workplace Program. "In those situations, the demands being placed on you exceed the resources you have available to deal with the stressors."

For many female principals, we are not aware of the signs we should look for to begin to take action once the signs of burnout have shown up. According to Forbes, they list seven signs that burnout exists; I will discuss three of these signs:

EXHAUSTION

Exhaustion is the sense of not having any energy or feeling tired all the time. This feeling can be emotional, physical or mental.

LACK OF MOTIVATION

Lack of Motivation happens when you begin noticing that you are not as excited about the job as you once were. This could also be a sign of burnout. When you lack a desire to get ready for work or you begin to frequently call out sick for work, these may also show as signs of a lack of Motivation.

FRUSTRATION, CYNICISM AND OTHER NEGATIVE EMOTIONS

Suddenly becoming a negative "nancy" or feeling like the work you are doing doesn't matter might reflect a change in emotions. Becoming overly frustrated with systems and confines of the work, with no sign of resolve, can become manifestations in one's behavior.

HOW TO AVOID BURNOUT

If you have noticed that you have already begun to experience some signs of burnout, or you simply want to avoid burnout as a female principal, consider the ways to eliminate or avoid additional stress that are listed below:

WORK LIFE BALANCE

As as administrator, It is important to create a healthy work life balance in order to maintain focus. Work life balance is what I consider an harmonious blend of work and play. It is the between of being on your "grind" and laying low. It is the "rub" between hustle and flow. A healthy work life balance allows you to make the cake and have the time to eat the cake. Work life balance is important because it helps you to avoid burnout. If you are not resting, recouping and revamping, you will find yourself working in overdrive, and that cannot be sustained. Knowing how demanding leadership is, you need to ensure that you have time to relax, rest, keep up with family and have some fun. When you are not working, build your personal life by enjoying your hobbies. Do some workouts to rejuvenate your body. Being confined at work can be depressing. You have to make sure you release that stress regularly. Engaging in these activities will help you achieve balance and happiness in your life.

TAKE OWNERSHIP OF YOUR CALENDAR

One quick way to hit burnout is by not managing your calendar. You must become the master of your calendar and your time. As a principal, It is easy to hit the ground running and begin working nonstop. The moment you are assigned to your new school the excitement is overwhelming, and you begin to work nonstop in preparing for the opening of school. You prepare to meet the staff to plan for the upcoming year, and you, quickly, find out that there doesn't seem to be enough time in the day to get everything done. Many tasks have to be completed during the work day; therefore, it is important to manage your calendar and master your time. Be reminded of the importance of incorporating what you need to do for yourself.

Take Action- Generate the top five things you need to do for yourself. It is important to create your list so that you allow time to focus on yourself. You can become so involved in your role as principal and forget about your needs. Open your calendar (use Outlook calendar, and other phone or electronic calendar aps) and create a monthly, standing appointment. Create the time for the things you have to do for yourself. Making and keeping these appointments should be a priority.

Here is a list of my favorite things to do:

LINE · DANCING/ZUMBA
SCANDAL · TV WATCHING
MASSAGE · THERAPY
PEDICURES · HAIR APPOINTMENTS

I enjoyed doing these things for myself, and I scheduled these activities in advance. I color coded them to stand out when I looked over my weekly/monthly agenda. It gave me something to look forward to, and it also kept me balanced.

KEEP TABS ON YOUR HEALTH

As a figure of power, you need to stay physically and mentally strong. You will have many duties, and some of them will be very challenging. Stress and physical strain are inevitable. A day in the life of a principal might include: attending a morning meeting, handling the daily routine, attending to guests and going to different places to get things done. Truthfully, not all guests, committee members, employees or shareholders are easy to get along with. Disagreements and collisions are bound to happen. Sometimes, these disagreements may be fueled by the fact that you are a lady in leadership with rank. By the end of the day, you might find that you are exhausted and your stamina diminished. It is important to keep track of how much rest you get.

At all costs, avoid taking those drugs that induce insomnia so that you can stay up all night working. You may think you are optimizing your effort or time, but you are causing damage to your body. Your performance will only worsen. Now and then, take healthy food and some water for a lunch break to fuel your body and to enhance your energy level It is advisable to include exercise in your schedules; exercise improves metabolism and brain activity. It enables you to stay in great shape and work energetically. While working, it is very beneficial to create a system that offers self-care to maintain your overall health.

MAKE FRIENDS

Now that you are a leader, do not commit the mistake of assuming that you are a loner. Unlike wolves, we human beings are social creatures, and we live co-dependently. After all, even the alpha needs his team. Under your supervision, you will be responsible for multiple roles, and you will need assistance. Make acquaintance with the workers and members of the school committee. You will be surprised how much they can teach you. Friends will also be your critics, and they will express the truth about strategies or suggestions. Making wise decisions will be based on different perceptions. When choosing associates, be careful because everyone won't be genuinely happy about your success. It is noteworthy to be prudent and assess advice; some of it can put you in trouble. Socializing with friends from the school and with people from other sectors can be helpful. Get to know people by attending conferences and events and be open to the ideas of others by listening to their stories. This not only builds your reputation, but you will learn some lessons about handling leadership.

MONITORING TIME

One of the most important elements in a principal's daily life is time. Remember the myriad of jobs awaiting your manipulation? There is a need to manage time as much as possible; therefore, it is most important to keep a schedule. Your schedule should include the activities you have on a certain day, the times and the approximate length of time of the activities. You may also add some important information, including who might be scheduled to appear. Other activities like deliveries and inspection should be included. Your schedule should act as a reminder of the things that need to be done, the people to be seen and the events to be attended each day. Most failures are caused by a lack of order and discipline in time management. The result of not accurately recording entries on your calendar could mean that, upon your arrival at work, your secretary has to inform you that you have missed an organized meeting by an hour. Such mishaps might be recorded on your record of good leadership and lead to the school manager's observations of you. Armed with a schedule, you will be able to counter all such incidents and avoid the stress that occurs when an important meeting is missed.

PERSONAL EXPERIENCE

Initially, I had uncertainty about writing this section. It is difficult to put into words the weakness and vulnerability we have as humans and leaders. As principals, the crisis and everyday battles are major aspects of our lives. As we protect and defend our children and the entire system, we can't deny that we have an internal struggle within our conscience. The fight is not just out there; it is within us. At times, especially when alone, it is easy to fall into that maze labeled "mental argument." This can really affect our performance as a leader and a nurturer. Therefore, the question remains, how do we combat this? We need first to identify signs that we are moving towards a burnout. What are these signs? Are they recognizable? How can we detect them? How can we avoid a burnout?

We are normally accustomed to believe that we must be fully committed to our children and the school. We sacrifice our personal freedom, time, effort and even resources to ensure that the students are comfortable. However, this starts to go south when we are no longer ready to fight. We, internally, raise our hands in surrender when we can no longer stand the pressure. Before I became a principal, I remember encountering people who had decided to give up their positions as principals. Their rationales for quitting revolved around spending more time with their families and being fed up with the politics. To me, this was a sign of weakness and a lack of determination. I judged them as quitters who would never have made it. However, when I became principal, I learned the bitter truth. I learned what it meant to be a leader who was depended upon for everything. I was on the brink of sacrificing their entire lives for the sake of work. I, then, understood the predicament of the retired principals. As my mentor always said, "People think they know more than the principal until they become the principal."

I recall suffering with burnout-silently and alone. I couldn't bring myself to face that something was *off* with my level of enthusiasm. At the end of the school year, I had a conversation with my mentor who was able to determine my level of passion for most things. She simply asked me, "How happy are you with the work you are doing." I attempted to be calm when I answered her question. I explained the terrific pace at which I had to do things and push my staff while it still felt like nothing was changing. My emotions spilled, and I cried. I was exhausted. I was working twice as hard as the rest, but they seemed to be improving while I was stagnated at one point. It was tiring and frustrating to work all the time and have poor results.

The words of wisdom my mentor gave me that day calmed me and ignited a new and positive viewpoint. She advised me to be true to myself. As a principal, this advice will fill your cup when nothing else will. Knowing that you are doing what is best for you, your staff and your students is a surefire way to keep you grounded in good times and in times of development.

COPING WITH BURNOUT

REJUVENATING YOUR PASSION

What happens when you lose passion for your work? Being burned out is a problem. If you have lost focus or morale for doing your job as a principal, it will not take long before you are out of will power. Therefore, you need to work your motivation issues. Ask yourself questions. Am I still passionate about my work? Why is my morale low? What can I do to remedy this? If you fail to identify the problem early and fast enough, it is game over for you.

Once you identify the reason why you are losing focus, work to solve these problems. A helpful way is to revisit your initial goals of pursuing this role. What did you aim to achieve and how far are you at succeeding? Your basic objectives can reinvigorate your passion. Finally, decide on your stand. Are you still passionate about this job? This will help you be assertive about continuing with the job with vigilance and excellence.

Being a leader means having a lot of responsibility. The person for that job has to be strong enough to handle it. Therefore, as a principal, you must ensure that your health, time, social skills and passion are aligned with the job. If this is your reality, your propensity to prosper will increase significantly.

WORK IN YOUR WHEELHOUSE.

Often times, we can reset our love for our jobs by spending time focusing on the parts of our jobs that we enjoy. I love professional development, coaching, and training adults. When I found it difficult to stay focused on the job, I would pull out our professional development calendar and begin brainstorming ideas for developing trainings and ways to reach staff. I didn't allow this to replace the work that had to be done. By doing this practice, it allowed me to be refocused and excited about other areas of work, because they are connected. Delegating tasks to develop leadership capacity in your building can be an effective way to share duties and responsibilities. When a principal has an opportunity to observe projects as they come to life from a different, professional angle, creativity can be sparked and a reconnection to the work, at hand, can happen.

RECONNECT WITH YOUR "WHY".

Pull out your journals and your notes about why you became a principal. Do you still want this? Get real about your desire to continue being a principal. Do you still want your same environment? Are the reasons you want to stay in the position enough to keep you employed and connected for six to nine months? Can you finish the school year? Remember that people deserve to have the best school leaders, and they also deserve to have the best you show up for yourself daily.

MAKE A DECISION.

You have to be honest with yourself by identifying the problem and finding a strategy to keep you in the game. Ask yourself the tough questions and determine your commitment level in your position. Make a decision to stay in the position with assistance or to make a career move. Recognizing the signs of burnout and taking action quickly will help you to make the appropriate decisions that are right for you versus having a supervisor making the decision for you, based on poor job performance.

TIPS & FINAL TAKEAWAYS

Learn the signs of burnout and remember the ways to avoid it. Take care of yourself to continue to be the most effective principal you can be. Remember to be true to yourself and make the best decision for you. It will serve you and your staff well in the long run.

FOR READERS

1. What are the things you do for regular self-care?

_____
_____
_____
_____
_____
_____
_____
_____

2. What steps can you take to avoid burnout?

_____
_____
_____
_____
_____
_____
_____
_____
_____
_____

Chapter 3:

THE DIFFERENT FACES OF FEMALE LEADERSHIP:

WHEN YOU ARE DIFFERENT, YOU LEAD DIFFERENTLY

CHANGE BRINGS DIFFERENCE

I HAVE ALWAYS HAD strong dreams of becoming a powerful leader. After I noticed how effective I was in teaching and managing affairs, I decided I wanted to be a school principal. I was twenty four years old, and I didn't have any family responsibilities. It was my time to pursue my aspirations. I was an active participant in district meetings, workshops and other programs. I was a strong-willed leader who mastered all aspects of leadership. I moved to New Orleans to seek a bigger challenge in a school district other than the one where I was employed. I joined a training program for prospective principals, and I got a job as one, with no underlying responsibilities, I immersed myself fully into the new position. The school required so much work that it took days of the week to keep it on its feet. The duties suppressed even my ability to enjoy a break. My father succumbed to cancer, and my mother became critically ill. I still continued to work. I was absent on several birthdays, important events, and I lacked a relationship because I worked all of the time. This became my trend for a number of years, until it dawned on me that something was amiss. I didn't have a personal life. Even though I was well established, and my school was thriving, I had no strong social ties. I decided to change my approach to life and work, and things changed, fortunately, for the better. Since the transformation, I did not have the extra hours to spend working on school matters. My time has now been partitioned between work and my personal life. I socialized a lot more and became closer to my friends and family. This changed my social health and improved my personality, according to the employees. They admitted that I was growing more approachable, which was a great step for me. When I got my second job as a principal, things were different. I was more matured and had better experience in handling the job. I installed a totally different system from the one used on my first job. I understood the need of having a life outside of work.

A DIFFERENT TYPE OF LEADERSHIP.

When you are different, you lead differently. So many things in our personal life impact the work that we do and how we do the work. As human beings, we change and evolve multiple times in our lives. Changes in life shape our decision making in various areas, including our career. When I was younger, I wanted to be an attorney. As I got older, I changed my mind about my career, and I made a different choice. The differences that we face in our lives and the decisions we make become more personalized and individualized based on our circumstances. The differences that one encounters doesn't just impact one's personal decision. For principals, the decisions that they make can impact the leadership style that one develops.

AGE

They say old is gold. This is quite true but does not imply being younger is bad. Many young people are chasing their dreams of becoming great people. There is nothing wrong with that. However, as people grow older, they get better in some qualities. For instance, it is statistically true that older people are wiser. They may not have as much stamina, but their brain contains a lot of information. They become better at detecting patterns based on their lifetime encounters, and this makes them better decision makers, an important quality in a leader. Young people, on the other hand, are lively and have active cognitive abilities; however, they need to understand that learning takes time. As it relates to the principalship, your age may not necessarily dictate your ability to lead others, but your age may offer the opportunity to gain experiences that will assist you in leading others.

MARITAL STATUS

This aspect affects our lives more than we care to admit. As portrayed in the story, being a workaholic can be negative. It pushes you away from people since you have no more time for them. If you are married, this might drive a wedge between you and your spouse. If your system works to give you time for your loved ones, your relationship will have a better chance of survival. However, single people seem to have an easier time dealing with their lives. This, surprisingly, is not entirely true. Of course, you do not have another individual to worry about apart from yourself, but you are at an equal risk of severing your social life if you shut others out. Sadly, some accomplished people end up alone because they fail to establish their social lives in the name of work. Some choose to stay single; this is a personal choice. However, whether married or single, your system of leadership should be able to accommodate your spouse. The principalship can require time to become effective. The place you are in regarding your marital status does not determine your effectiveness as a principal, however it may impact your decision on timing for promotions, school types and additional roles.

PARENTHOOD

Becoming a parent is a great experience. However, with it comes a new bundle of energy that needs to be taken care of, nurtured and raised. Being a mother, as well as a principal, can be a daunting task for one person. Your entire schedule will have to be changed to accommodate your new responsibility. You will have to take more time to nurture your child, and you will need to give up the late nights for the sake of your child. Therefore, you will need strategies to balance work and family time in order to not abandon your roles and neither will you neglect your child or the children you see on the job. Being a parent also heightens your awareness of the needs of children, and it lets you know the parenting skills needed to be a better parent. You will probably become a more gentiler and friendlier you. Parenthood will increase your understanding of working with others, and it will highlight the needs for discipline, respect and excellence in the workplace. Parenthood means giving what you'd like to receive. Having a great support system is a wonderful addition for several female principals who are also parents. Family planning and child rearing are important to many female principals, and if you are a new parent, or planning on becoming a parent, the decisions you make will impact your career, principalship and leadership style.

EXPERIENCE

It is indeed the best teacher. Having the know-how of operating a school is a great advantage because you would have acquired the effective skills of transitioning and settling into an institution. Experience will teach you ways of maximizing your time as well as the skill of prioritizing to alleviate some common mistakes. During your time as principal, it is important to learn as much as you can so that you can improve and become more effective. The more you learn and apply, the better you become at the job, and you will build your reputation as an effective principal. It is very important for any leader to be effective and be seen as highly qualified in order to increase her chances of being selected for promotions or special projects.

EMOTIONAL STATUS

Having a load of responsibilities can take a toll on your emotional condition. Sometimes, you may be angered by something that went wrong, and you misplace your anger and your employees have to suffer from your wrath. This is wrong and unethical. Being extremely excited about something, especially personal, can also become problematic. As a leader, you should be considerate of the environment of your employees. Do not be rude or snappy to them as this lowers their morale. When you are in a good emotional state, it will positively impact the work that you are doing. Contrary to that, if you are not in a good emotional state, it will negatively impact your work and the work being done in the school environment. Your emotional status will determine the different decisions made about your work environment.

PHYSICAL ENERGY

Being a principal involves a lot of movement here and there and performing several duties all day. The role may not necessarily get the hands dirty, but it requires physical movement and energy. A physically fit individual is likely to be more efficient when compared with one with low energy. One may be low on energy due to a medical condition, physical tiredness or aging. The promptness of getting tasks done is essential in preventing being overwhelmed by work.

LOCATION

Location determines how available you are in case you are suddenly needed. For an anchored principal, this is good only if you stay in one school or schools within the vicinity. Floaters are often available since they settle close to the school.commuters are not a problem, and they get to work faster. More importantly, when there is an emergency, it is easier to summon them. Locating dwellers of a permanent home might be more difficult, especially if they have to shift to different schools now and then.

THE NEED TO REFLECT

It's important to know yourself and check in with yourself regularly and throughout the course of your career to know if you're changing and if your change matches your current work environment. For instance, ask yourself "are you the same person you were when you were the first year classroom teacher?" Now, compare yourself as a first-year classroom teacher to wherever you are on this journey for educational leadership. My guess is that you are very different, and your changes and your differences have indirectly and directly impacted your choices and your actions to this point. I recommend doing a reflection activity if you begin to notice change in your leadership areas. Pull out your journal or notebook, or you may even have a notebook that you've kept while dreaming of the principalship. Surely, you have been recording all of your bright ideas and visions you've had while in preparation. If so, pull that out too. Pulling out your past plans may help craft your blueprint for tomorrow. This reflection activity will allow you to gain focus and clarity on your changes and help you to make decisions on what is needed for you to continue to be an effective principal. To help you get your thoughts flowing during this reflection, use the guide below:

AGE YOU ENTERED EDUCATION: _____

JOB: _____

MARITAL STATUS: _____

LOCATION: _____

PRIORITIES: _____
_____
_____
_____

OUTLOOK ON EDUCATION: _____
_____
_____
_____

CAREER GOALS: _____
_____
_____
_____

OUTSIDE RESPONSIBILITIES: _____
_____
_____
_____

SATISFACTION WITH WORK: _____
_____
_____
_____
_____
_____
_____

Your age 3-7 years after your first job in education: _____

Job: _____

Marital Status: _____

Location: _____

Priorities: _____

Outlook on Education: _____

Career Goals: _____

Outside Responsibilities: _____

Satisfaction with Work: _____

Your age 7-10 years after your first job: _____
In education: _____
Job: _____
Marital Status: _____
Location: _____
Priorities: _____
_____
_____
_____

Outlook on Education: _____
_____
_____
_____

Career Goals: _____
_____
_____
_____

Outside Responsibilities: _____
_____
_____

Satisfaction with Work: _____
_____
_____
_____

What has changed in your life? How has your career changed? _____
_____

Your age 10-15 years after your first job in education: _____

Job: _____

Marital Status: _____

Location: _____

Priorities: _____

Outlook on Education: _____

_____

_____

_____

Career Goals: _____

_____

_____

_____

Outside Responsibilities: _____

_____

_____

_____

Satisfaction with Work: _____

_____

_____

_____

What has changed in your life? How has your career changed? _____

_____

_____

_____

_____

YOUR AGE 15-20 AFTER YOUR FIRST JOB
IN EDUCATION: _____
JOB: _____
MARITAL STATUS: _____
LOCATION: _____
PRIORITIES: _____
OUTLOOK ON EDUCATION: _____
_____
_____
_____

CAREER GOALS: _____
_____
_____
_____

OUTSIDE RESPONSIBILITIES: _____
_____
_____
_____

SATISFACTION WITH WORK: _____
_____
_____
_____
_____
_____
_____
_____
_____

This activity is tedious but worth the effort, and it will take you some time to complete it. No matter where you have been, it's healthy to stop and reflect to gain clarity on what's next and how you want the next phase to look. Collectively, your life events have played a role in your personal and professional development. As you complete this activity, do you have any lightbulb moments, when something about your educational career made perfect sense and was clear to you? Have you noticed that your focus has shifted? Are there any plans, goals or priorities that are similar across age groups? What goals and priorities do you still have? Do any of your goals, priorities clash with any areas of your work? What can you do today to change the level of satisfaction with your work?

FOUR LEADERSHIP STYLES

There are four major styles of leadership which are found in the educational setting.

SERVANT LEADERSHIP

places the end goal as a focus for the people being led. It embraces a no sense of self interest from the leaders as they support the interests of the followers with whom they trust.

TRANSACTIONAL LEADERSHIP

models a business transaction. It is a give and take model. Everyone involved gives something to get something.

EMOTIONAL LEADERSHIP

places concern on the feelings and motivations of the followers. Leaders motivate through emotional intelligence.

TRANSFORMATIONAL LEADERSHIP

emphasizes aligning values with the organization. Leaders are willing to take calculated risks by making informed decisions from team members.

As mentioned in a previous chapter, transformational leadership is becoming the desired leadership style for school systems, especially those with troubled school settings. In addition, female principals naturally have characteristics that make them great transformational leaders. Just because one leadership style may have once fit you doesn't mean that you don't adjust and take on different leadership styles.

For example, you may see a shift in leadership styles when the principal has been leading a school for a long period of time and has developed leaders and trust among the staff. This leader may shift to servant leadership where there is complete trust in the followers who are well aligned with the goal. The leader provides guidance and empowerment during the process.

The opposite can happen when a novice principal, who lacks the same level of experience, enters as a servant leader and realizes through experience that a shift in leadership style is needed. Becoming a transformational leader will require more hands on and inclusion.

CHANGE HAPPENS

What happens when you change and shift your leadership style or leadership focus?

When you are initially establishing yourself as a leader, crafting and identifying your leadership style can be difficult. It's important to give yourself the flexibility to change as you change over time. Your leadership style will change and be different as you become different. Recognize that change is okay and being different is allowed. However, when you're leading others, don't miss this important step: inform those working with you that a change is happening. When we miss this step, confusion arises, and people find it difficult to exhibit trust.

TIP & FINAL TAKEAWAYS:

Take inventory of yourself....

Ask yourself how different you are today from the time you began your career as a principal. All those differences are the changes that made you a better person. They also improve your leadership style. Whether your leadership style is transformational, strategic, team, cross-cultural, facilitative or even laissez-faire type, a change in your system is important to transforming the dynamics of your field into something better.

FOR READERS:

1. What things are you currently experiencing that would cause you to lead differently?

_____
_____
_____
_____
_____
_____
_____

2. How would others describe your leadership style? Would they say the same in 6 months?

_____
_____
_____
_____
_____
_____
_____

Chapter 4:
GIRL POWER: LEADING MEN

*E*VERYONE HAS BIASES, including principals. We are all human, but it's important to remember that we need to check those biases, especially in roles of leadership. When I first became a principal, I can recall that there wasn't an assistant principal at the school. The school had had several different acting principals. From my understanding, different people had worked in pseudo leadership positions in the absence of a true, dedicated principal. It was also my first year, and I hadn't even determined my true leadership style. I was a complete novice. I recall talking to my supervisor, who was giving me free reign to make my own decisions; however, she made some strong suggestions regarding the assistant principal's position. Her recommendation was to hire a male. I cringed at the thought of a male assistant principal because I felt that given the lack of leadership in the school building prior to my coming there as the principal, that people would automatically lean to a male for their directives versus me as the principal because I was a female. In essence, I must have felt that I would be inferior to a male administrator, even though I held the highest title in the school. How foolish I was! I was embarrassed with myself to have had these internal thoughts. Being truthful, I was afraid to have a male assistant principal. I hadn't had any problems giving directives to male teachers or other male support staff, but the idea of having a male assistant with me every single day made me a nervous. I wasn't sure if I could trust a male in that position. I questioned whether or not the male administrator would really follow my lead. Let's face it, if they desired to be an administrator, they must want to be the boss. What negative and closed-minded thinking I had. These feelings were stemming from my internal thoughts, biases and insecurities. I passed on hiring a male administrator; I just felt like I wasn't ready. As I have reflected on that experience, I regret having made that decision because I deprived my students of the opportunity to see a male in leadership. I also deprived myself of an opportunity to challenge my thinking.

Over the years, I learned that leading men is just like leading anyone else. It starts with you as the leader. You must be confident in your leadership abilities. If you're confident in your leadership abilities, you should be able to lead anyone. The first thing you have to do is identify your strengths and weaknesses and then check your biases at the door. Accept the fact that men and women respond to things differently. Your job as a good leader is to identify what individuals need and respond accordingly.

The challenges that women face, when dealing with men, often stem from our own insecurities and in some cases past experiences. You may be worried about how you're being perceived, or you worry about coming across as bitchy, or too strong. Maybe, you don't feel comfortable leading men working on your team. When I first became a principal, I felt many of these things, but I quickly learned that appropriately leading both genders is a key element for career success.

TIPS FOR LEADING MEN:

COMMUNICATE EFFECTIVELY

Be direct, Get to the point.

Men work well on teams when they know their position and the role they are expected to play. In the education setting, men respond when they are given a role, and they can explore the parameters and expectations of their role. In order to make this successful, you must be able to explain what your expectations are in a clear and concise manner. Be direct! Men value what you have to say when you say it with directedness. Avoiding excessive and unnecessary information. When giving redirects, cut straight to the point and avoid asking guiding questions. Remember, you don't want your messages to be lost like the teacher character from Charlie Brown Wah wah wah. You want your male employees to be able to fully understand what they are to do and how to be successful with the tasks you have given them.

BE AUTHENTIC

It's never a good look to pretend to be someone you are not. This is especially true in the principalship. People can usually see right through a fake persona, and this will make it difficult for you to build trust. When leading men, don't try to lead like a man. Steve Harvey's book title Act Like a Lady, Think Like a Man should become sort of a mantra for you when it comes to leading the men on your team. As a female leader, you have great leadership traits that you can utilize to be successful when leading others. You have been empowered with intuition, empathy, compassion, adaptability and tenacity. Continue to always be who you are and be proud of your female leadership traits, while realizing how men think.

BE ASSERTIVE

Contrary to popular belief, men actually respect a woman who can speak her mind and challenge things. Have you ever observed a group of men talking about the latest football game? No one is being polite and asking for permission to speak. Those men with opposing viewpoints don't sit quietly holding their opinions to themselves, afraid of what the other men in the group are going to think. Men want to hear your voice and your point of view, even if they don't' agree. As a principal, who is leading men, remember to be assertive and let your voice be heard in order to garner respect from the men on your team. Jump into that conversation, add your voice and don't wait for permission to be heard.

EMBRACE DIFFERENCES

Men are often motivated by goals and the possibility of achieving those goals, while women are often more process focused. As the principal, utilize these differences to help you achieve your school wide goals. Make your goals clear and visible to the team, and the males on your team will have a higher probability of being motivated to help you reach the goals. Allow them to contribute to the team. Once males have set goals, you can utilize their competitive nature to drive others around them to conquer those goals as well.

ADJUST EXPECTATIONS

Every classroom you visit will not be identical in design. Each teacher will bring a personal style into the classroom with colors, decor and theme. How many times have you walked into a male teacher's classroom and fell in love with his Little Mermaid themed classroom? Probability is that you haven't. I have never met a female principal who didn't have expectations of a warm and inviting classroom environment. But what does that mean for the male teacher who wears the same khaki pants and plaid shirt to work daily? What are the true expectations? Is it that each classroom will be decorated with over the top themes and ornaments from the craft store, or do you have specific elements that need to be in place? I have grown to expect that there are required elements that need to be visible in classrooms. Visuals might include posted objectives, students' work, and homework stations are desirable. Classrooms should be neat, orderly and free of clutter and debris. Conveying my expectations to the men on my team provided the opportunity to help them feel like their minimalist classroom would be acceptable.

USING OUR POWER FOR GOOD

We can't discuss leading men without discussing the male educator shortage that exists. While it is important, as a female leader, to know how to lead men, we play an important role in reversing the teacher shortage that exists among male teachers. According to the consortium for policy research in education, only about 24 percent of all teachers were male in 2012, with just one in 10 men teaching elementary students.

It is necessary to have men in the workplace in education because students need to see multiple examples of different types of people teaching and leading them, including ethnicity, class and gender. The school and classrooms have become a microcosm of our society. Many students are seldom faced with having a male teacher, and this can greatly impact the thoughts about how gender plays into careers. Having such a disparity of men in the teaching roles, continues to create a mindset that teaching is believed to be a role better suited for women, especially elementary teaching. This mindset, while highly concentrated at the elementary level, seems to create the same stigma associated with teaching in general.

We know that boys and girls learn differently, and if we, as principals, are committed to the academic success of all students, we must ensure that our hiring practices are in line with our belief. When the opportunities for hiring male teachers is consistently absent, we must begin to use our expertise, as school leaders, to change this.

When speaking with dozens of men about the how to adequately recruit and retain effective male teaches, surprisingly, many men didn't mention salary as one would expect. Instead, they mentioned the need to feel included in the process of change in a school. They did not want to feel like they would get stuck dealing with behavior problems. They want a principal who would take the time to hear what they need to be successful. Overall, men want to feel involved, and they want to teach and reach children on an academic level. They see themselves serving in the role of a mentor; they just need to be given the opportunity.

HOW CAN FEMALE PRINCIPALS SHIFT THE ATMOSPHERE?

Female principals must begin and stay connected to the conversation around the importance of having men in education. This includes how we lead men, as well as recruitment and retention of qualified male applicants. We must also figure out ways to lead men based on their interests and teaching style without compromising ourselves or the expectations.

Request male interns from local universities. These institutions are working on supply and demand. College of education departments are looking for ways to produce the best teaching candidates. Often times the heads of these departments are meeting with someone in your district! Find out who that person is and start saying what you want and what you're looking for. If that doesn't work, you can begin to have conversations with people at local colleges and universities. Let's face it, you are the principal, and you can get what you want. Host your own meet and greet/tour session of your school and invite local male organizations. Start with any volunteer organizations you currently work with to hear about your school and possible alternative ways to get into the teaching field.

TIPS & FINAL TAKEAWAYS:

Check your personal biases about leading men. Remember that your key to career success is learning how to successfully lead all people. The students you serve need to see teachers of all genders to positively shape their outlook on the world and you have the power to positively impact that.

FOR READERS:

1. What are some of your biases you have regarding managing men?

2. Do you find leading men a challenge?

3. What strategies are you using or plan to use to recruit and retain men in schools?

Chapter 5:
FINDING THE RIGHT FIT:

ACCEPTING THE RIGHT POSITION AND WHY IT MATTERS MOST TO WOMEN

The title of *principal* is exciting to many people, and sometimes the excitement of attaining the title without a clear understanding of the demands of the role can be misleading. In these instances, leaders can find themselves accepting a position prematurely or one that is not the right fit personally.

Finding the right fit starts with knowing who you are and what you want. It is similar to a relationship. Being able to partner with someone else, requires you to really know who you are, individually, before you pair with someone else. The same is true for the principalship. Before getting deeply into finding the right fit with a principal job, let's spend some time taking a look at you to determine if YOU are the right fit. Let's get clear on why you really want to be a principal. To do this, we will work with framing questions. Framing Questions will allow you to honestly analyze yourself. Hold a mirror up to your face for the purpose of framing and focusing your thoughts to get a deeper understanding of you.

START BY ASKING YOURSELF THESE 4 FRAMING QUESTIONS:

1. Why do you want to lead?
2. Are you ready to lead?
3. Do you have the time to lead?
4. Do you have a support team?

FRAMING QUESTION #1: WHY DO YOU WANT TO LEAD?

Are you excited about the increase in salary? Have others told you you would make a great leader? Do you want to be the principal because you enjoy helping others? Have you always found yourself in leadership roles in the past?

There are a million reasons to explain your desire to lead, to be the principal; however, the reasons are not always the best reasons nor are the reasons tied to the reality that the principalship is hard work. Many people are in love with the idea of being a principal, but just like the saying goes… all that glitters is not gold. You must have a realistic idea of what the principalship really is. A realistic view of the principalship, coupled with your honest reason why you want to lead, will help you avoid accepting the wrong position.

Remember, the framing exercise only works if you are honest with yourself. There are so many reasons why people decide they want to go into the principalship. First, many people, if they're honest with themselves, are attracted to the principalship for the glitz and the glam that they "think" that the principalship caries. Let's be real, teacher and principal salaries are available to view online for almost any school district in the United States. It's no secret that there are, oftentimes, a major difference in the salary of a teacher and a principal. It is also no mystery that teachers, in America, earn signafitly lower salaries as compared to other degree holding professionals. Many people are excited about the idea of earning more money in their current field and immediately decide that they want to become a principal. I'm going to tell you right now that if that is your number one reason why you want to be a principal, do yourself a favor and find another option. Salary alone will not be enough to sustain you in the work of the principalship. Sometimes, the reason to start a position is not always the same reason that helps us to remain in the position. Maybe, the principalship was attractive due to the salary increase, however, the passion for changing students' lives is what keeps you from resigning when the superintendent calls a late afternoon meeting the day before your vacation. Yes, that actually happens. What drives you? What will sustain you? Do you want to help transform the face of education? There is no right or wrong answer when asked why you want to lead; you simply have to know the answer and be confident in your answer. What is your why?

FRAMING QUESTION: #2: ARE YOU READY TO LEAD?

The better question is—are you ready to lead as the principal? You may have been in leadership roles in the past, however the the principal position is the ultimate leadership position in a school building. Take a look at how you have led in the past. Are you good at leading a difficult team? How have you handled push back? Are you a self starter?

There is no magic formula or timetable that can tell you that you are ready to become a principal. I know really great principals that were classroom teachers for three years. I know really awesome principals that were assistant principals for half a semester, and I know really awesome principals that were teachers for fifteen years, then served as assistant principals for ten years. There is no magic timetable that says that a person is or is not ready to be a principal; however, there are qualities and attributes that one must have to be successful in the principal's role. For example, you cannot be ready to be a principal if you have not had a dramatic mindset shift. When asking yourself if you're ready to be a principal, ask yourself about your level of professionalism; ask yourself about your level of dedication. You might also ask yourself if you are thinking like a principal. I have found that when you are excited about the opportunity to be the principal, you have already begun to have tons of ideas on things you would do when you finally get to the position. You begin by creating files and documents you think might be handy in your new role. Some people even think about what type of team they may need to have in order to do the job effectively. People, who are thinking this way, tend to be excellent forward thinkers, which is a great quality to have as a principal. Waiting to think about ideas after you are appointed is too late! Be ready, so you won't have to get ready!

I hear these responses when I ask people if they are ready to be be a principal: I'm already doing the work of a principal, and I'm practically running the building. I've been an assistant principal for _X_ number of years. You may even have said them yourself; I know that I did. I am here to tell you that you may think that as a assistant principal you are doing the principal's work; however, that is far from the truth. As an assistant principal, you may be managing teachers; you may be responsible for the budget; you may be overseeing staff members; you may be leading common planning, and the list goes on, but there is an additional support system in place. It's a scaffolded level of leadership, and it's a safety net that exists in that role. You may not recognize it, but once you step into the role of a principal, you immediately recognize that there had been a safety net all along. Now, you are expected to perform and walk that tightrope without it, and it can be SCARY. In the principalship, the responsibility and accountability are different from those of an assistant principal, teacher or as a coach. There is no safety net; there is no one else, it is all on you. As the principal you are up at night, you set the vision, the goals, and you drive the ship. You are not waiting for directives; you are making multiple decisions daily, and you carry the sole reputation of the school building.

Are you ready for walking the tightrope without the safety net? Can you handle the pressure?

When She Leads

Framing Question #3:
Do You Have Time to Lead?

Do you have time to be the principal? Are you thinking that once you are a principal you will have a more flexible schedule? Are you thinking that you'll finally be able to make after school appointments? Let's face it; you can go to the restroom whenever you want! ! ! ! ! ! ! ! ! ! ! What an amazing educator perk! When I became a principal, I found out that I had a more flexible schedule, and I had the luxury to pop in and out of things at my leisure. I also recognized that there were more responsibilities on my plate, which meant that I spent more hours working. In fact, I wasn't able to be the first person to leave in the afternoons. My personal, dismissal plans were often delayed because there were situations that needed to be handled by an administrator, and this has often left me, the principal, to handle those situations. .

As a principal, you must understand that having time to lead means that, oftentimes, you are devoting weekends, afternoon hours, and early morning hours to make sure that you are getting things done, because during the school day, you simply can't get it all done. After hours work for principals include: typing up administrative observation notes, typing memos and newsletters for staff, following up with emails and parent concerns and your school-based planning needs. Actually, most principals find that they are spending the same after work hours that were once preserved for grading papers and lesson planning. If you lead a very active after school lifestyle, sometimes, that means that you must alter your schedule so that you can get things done. Working after hours will help you avoid taking work home and allow you time to devote yourself to other areas outside of work.

It's important to think about the personal requirements you have outside of school and how they impact the amount of energy you can put into the job as a principal. Honestly, no one cares about your after school duties, and no one else will take things home with them. No one cares if you have a babysitter that cancelled; no one's going to care if you have a sick parent at home that you are responsible for. No one cares, and no one's going to show you empathy for having these extra responsibilities that go on in your life that may impede on the time that you're able to give as a principal. As a principal, you must always remember that you cannot give what you don't have. If you do not have time to invest in the work, that can become problematic. When you think about time, keep in mind that various school types will require different time allotments for principals. For example, if you are working in a challenging school that has not been run effectively for previous years, you can anticipate a large time commitment to turn a particular school around. When thinking about time, think about the level of experience that you are bringing to the table. When you are a new principal, it is very easy to devote a lot of your time out of your afternoon activities into becoming the principal that you want to be. Learning a new skill is a huge learning curve when you're entering the role of a new principal, and that learning curve requires additional time out of your day. If you struggle with time in other positions, I can guarantee you that you're going to struggle with time as the principal. In order to manage your time well, you have to make sure you have systems in place and allowed time necessary to devote to the job.

If you are currently observing other principals and you are making assumptions about the amount of time they are putting into the job, consider various factors. For one, consider the amount of years that that particular principal has been in the role. Second, consider the type of school that the principal is overseeing. Third, consider the amount of time that that principal has been at that particular school. All of these things can drastically affect the amount of time that you will have to invest. Seasoned principals, who has been at schools for many years, may find that they are spending less outside time investing into their role because they have gotten effective at it. They have learned shortcuts, and they have built teams. They don't have to spend a lot of time learning or trying new things. An additional learning curve exists with a novice principal who has to learn the role of the principal and the roles of the inherited teams. Additional time will have to be invested in role and team development. Over time, that same novice principal may find that she is using less of her outside time as systems become more automatic inside the school. Identify your level of organization.

Being a principal and the leader means that you have to have time to listen and to hear concerns from students, teachers, staff members, parents and the community. As a principal, you can spend anywhere from two hours or more in meetings just listening to concerns. Being able to carve out the time to listen, knowing that those concerns are valid, can help you to change the overall culture and climate of your school. Taking the time to listen is important but also time consuming. Having an open door policy is standard, but you must have limitations- times when you are available to truly listen to the people that you serve. Do you struggle with carving out time for tasks? Identify your level of organization, and if this is a problem area for you, it must be addressed prior to the principalship.

FRAMING QUESTION #4: DO YOU HAVE A SUPPORT TEAM?

It doesn't matter if you are single with no children, married, divorced, or raising a family of five, everyone needs an outside support team while in the principalship. How you develop your support team is entirely up to you, but it should be based on your individual needs. However, there are some examples of who should be a part of your support team.

THE SHOULDER TO CRY ON

The person you can yell, unravel and scream with.

Having this person, as a member of your team, will allow you to have someone who will listen to your venting and yelling. As a principal, you will need a shoulder to cry on in order to get through the challenging times. As human beings, it is healthy for us to be able to express our feelings. The kind of person you select will make a difference; therefore, you should choose a person who is empathetic and will listen to you when you want to talk about: how bad your day was, how much your boss may be getting on your nerves, or how the teachers are not quite doing exactly what you want them to do. You can go to this person, not necessarily for advice, but just to have a safe space to be yourself and vent out your frustrations and emotions. The person in this role may or may not be able to give you advice on how to make the job better or how to make changes; you may not even need this person for that reason. Be advised that you will need a safe, confidential place where you can show your emotions, be yourself and say what you are feeling. You can select a close family member, a friend, coach or mentor as your "go to person." They may or may not know what to say to make the situation better, but they are there to listen and a offer a shoulder to cry on. Be careful if this is a family member or close friend, they tend to not be the person to "push" us when times are difficult. Coaches and mentors can be very helpful.

THOUGHT PARTNER

A thought partner on your support team can be extremely fun and energizing. This person is someone with whom you can brainstorm your ideas and visions. Your thought partner can be a colleague or someone who has done similar work. As you make plans for your school, you will need someone who can assist you by listening, making suggestions and offering encouragement. It will be helpful to have a thought partner who can motivate you, provide a spark to your creativity, and help you make any adjustments in any plans that you may have. Your thought partner will assist you in analyzing potential problems to help you avoid any pitfalls in your plan. A thought partner is also great to have because the partnership will allow you to share feedback, especially if your partner is doing the same work. Your thought partner may also be a person with whom you feel safe and can share your frustration. If you and your thought partner are principals, you will be doing similar projects and setting similar goals. You and your thought partner should be committed to taking action by getting right to the source of the concerns and immediately working with each other to fix problems and avoid pitfalls. Have fun, avoid complaining, be amicable and enjoy the partnership.

A CHEERLEADER

A cheerleader is someone who thinks you're great! She is someone who will celebrate you when you're up and cheer you on when you're down. This is the person who stands on the sidelines of your work and cheers you along as she watches you perform. You will need someone who will be encouraging and remind you why you started this process. Give careful thought to the person who could be your cheerleader because your cheerleader must be your choice. It could be that person who told you about your greatness and encouraged you to finish the master's program. When you are doubting yourself, the cheerleader can be the person who helps you feel like you can conquer the world. Educational leaders will tell you that they are in the most thankless job. Principals have to have "tough" skin, and, oftentimes, they get conditioned to not receiving praise, thank yous or pats on the back. At the end of the day, they are human beings who need to be appreciated and celebrated. When you feel defeated, the cheerleader, on your support team, will be the person who won't let you be too hard on yourself. An excellent cheerleader will encourage and support you when everyone else seems to be against you. Cheerleaders are genuine, loyal, and they will praise you and believe in you and your abilities. They will help you hold a mirror to your image to show you your greatness. Your cheerleader can be anyone who will give you a dose of reality filled with love and support. They might show up as members of your think tank or thought partners team to lend support, offer suggestions and serve as encouragers. My two cheerleaders were a close friend and my mother. Both of these people were extremely helpful, and they gave me words of advice that were irreplaceable and invaluable. They helped me sustain myself through the years of my principalship by reminding me why I started the challenge of being a principal. Cheerleaders will be there for you when you think you can't do it, when your plans fail, or when you don't meet your goals, and they will remind you to stay the course. They intervene with you and help you avoid "beating up" on yourself. When the test scores at my school were returned, and they were lower than I expected, my two cheerleaders helped me by encouraging me to avoid any negative, self talk. I remember saying things like "maybe I'm not cut out for this job", or " I just can't do it". My cheerleaders reminded me of other accomplishments I had made and offered scriptures and affirmations regarding success and goals. This support was genuine and motivating and something that helped me to mentally get back on track.

A MENTOR

I am a strong believer in the Mentor/Mentee Relationship. I believe that every great principal should have a mentor and should themselves mentor others. As a principal, mentoring others will help you to develop other great female leaders, which is discussed in Girl Code, and it will help you develop as you have the opportunity to reflect about your experiences and share them. A mentor is someone who takes a personal interest and forms a relationship with you. When choosing a mentor, seek someone who will take this relationship seriously and who will have a vested interest and commitment to your success as a principal. Your mentor should be honest, approachable and available. In addition, a strong mentor is objective and fair when giving feedback and insight. Mentors help you to see areas of improvement that might stimulate your personal and professional growth. Mentors can serve in many capacities; therefore, they can bring a wealth of knowledge to your support team. Having a dedicated person to serve in the mentorship role, will help to provide balance within your support team and give you the opportunity to have multiple voices of support. Typically, a mentoring relationship will develop and grow through your current work. The mentoring relationship should not be a forced relationship.

A COACH

A coach functions similar to a mentor in approach and skills. A coach will offer a shorter term of support and is often task-based.

A coach will teach you relevant skills, tactictics and techniques. The purpose of the coach is to help you improve, and once this is done, the coach is no longer needed. Coaches are typically called upon when a person is not meeting expectations or is struggling with tasks. From the onset, it is advisable to identify a coach to be a member of your support team. A coach, on your support team, will help you in areas where you may struggle. She can help you in analyzing data, culture building and public speaking. A coach is different from a mentor in that she pushes you when it's needed, trains and guides you during the process, identifies your weaknesses and helps you understand the procedures of your role as a principal. You can receive coaching from a variety of ways, including virtual, group, individual, or in person. Your needs will determine what style is best suited for you. Many school districts do not provide the right amount of principalship coaching; therefore, you may need to seek an outside person to serve as your coach. Find a person who is credible and has a track record of helping others to be successful. Your professional memberships, and online groups like facebook, instagram and linkedin are all great resources to find a great coach.

Keep in mind that all of these roles may overlap, and you may have people who have multiple roles in your system. It is important to make sure that you have someone to help you when you need it. Just remember to have people in your corner who are going to keep it genuine and be there to support you as you serve as the leader in a school. .

Imagine yourself receiving an award for the Principal of the Year. You have had an amazing school year, of changing culture, building relationships, and student achievement. You are so happy and excited about the work you have done! You are overjoyed that YOU are being recognized! As you picture yourself standing on the dais to receive your award and you begin to offer thanks to your amazing support team—Who are those people? Who makes you great? Those are the people you make a part of your support team

When you are eager to land your first leadership position, it is important to not just chose anything. Maybe, you have been dreaming of the promotion for several years. Maybe, you have been wishing for your time to finally get the keys to any school building and park in that coveted Principal's Only parking space. However, you want to make sure that you are in a school that is the best fit for YOU. Accepting the wrong job offer can not only cause stress, but it can derail or ruin your career from the onset.

My first principalship was located in a small town I'd never visited or heard of. I felt that I was in a place in my career where I was ready for the principalship, and I was going to get it by any means necessary. I also felt like I wasn't getting appointed quickly enough in my current school district. I began looking for principalship positions outside of my home area; I was opened to moving and relocating. I was contacted about a small school district in need of a school principal; I applied on a whim and hoped for the best. I didn't know anything about the school district, or the community. Once I received the call to interview for the job, I began researching the school I was hoping to lead, and I found that the testing scores for the school were listed. I began doing a data dive to determine some possible gaps in the achievement levels. I created a plan to increase student performance. The teachers and staff were invited to a panel interview when I presented my plan, and they loved it! When I interviewed, my plan was applauded and accepted, and I just knew that I was going to be their new principal. During my previous years of experience, I had been heavily focused in an urban, educational setting, but I was really ready to change my setting, and this school seemed perfect. The socioeconomic makeup of the school was an equal balance by races, ethnicities, cultures and socio economic statuses, and they were only a few points away from earning a B school rating. Later that day, the assistant superintendent contacted me to let me know how impressed the staff was and that they voted for me to be their next principal. I was eager and excited to get started; however, something happened. A new principal vacancy was posted and after a few days of playing phone tag and several unanswered emails, the assistant superintendent called me again. She was still anxious to get me into her district, but there was another school that recently needed a principal. I, instantly, knew what was happening. She continued to say that the new school was a bit "challenged" and that the district team noticed that I had extensive experience in "challenged" settings. She was telling me that I would be a perfect for that school. She went on to advise me that I simply needed to change a few slides in my plan and be prepared to meet the staff of the other school. I knew deep down that I wanted a different setting, but I was so eager to get the title of principal that I moved forward with the process. I only had limited information on the school that had earned an "F" school rating and had a large population of students on free or reduced lunch. It was the lowest performing school in the district. Again, the staff loved me and voted me as their principal, and I accepted the offer. I was hired five days before the teachers were scheduled to return. I didn't have an office staff; I didn't have an assistant principal, and the school had one vacancy left to fill. It was imperative for me to immediately relocate. Soon after I accepted the position, I met with the Human Resources Department to discuss my salary. I was appalled! The salary I was offered was less than my previous position and comparable with an assistant's salary from my home district. Later, I would learn that the salary schedules hadn't been readjusted due to the discourse that existed with the new superintendent. I still accepted the position. During my first meeting with my supervisor, I asked three questions: How do I hire and fire? How do we spend money? and What is the quick and dirty on the curriculum? With only five days before I was to meet the staff, I didn't have a lot of time to learn the history of the school; however, I was still eager and excited to get to work as the PRINCIPAL. I recall the feeling I had when I pulled up to the school for the first time and seeing my name on the marque welcoming me as the new principal; I was thrilled! Needless to say, this was a very challenging year for me. I felt like it took me months to get a handle on many things, including operations and community relations. I realized that the start of my challenges came from the major mistakes I made during my appointment as a new principal. I failed to ask the right questions. I failed to talk to the right people, and I made assumptions about the community that I was serving. I hope you will learn from my experience. This was a true account of my experience and what I have learned. As you begin your job as a principal and your journey into principalship, let my experience help you in identifying the school that is the right fit for you. Remember to:

ASK THE RIGHT QUESTIONS:

GET TO KNOW WHY YOU ARE HIRED.

Questions to ask yourself before being offered the principalship:

- What do I need to know about the previous administration?
- What are the expectations of the principal?
- What are the reasons YOU were hired?

IDENTIFY YOUR TYPE:

Do you have a passion for working with students who are in a low socioeconomic location? Do you vision running a small boutique school with a large PTA? Are you interested in the charter world or start up? These are all questions you should ask yourself when you are pursuing leadership positions. If you are not equipped to work with challenging students, you may not want to accept a job in a low socio economic setting or in a state turnaround setting. The best way to identify your type is to inventory the types of schools you have worked in in the past. Determine what type of school it was and rate your effectiveness and your job satisfaction level. Then, look for positions with similar demographics and design makeup. The following chart will help you make a determination:

SCHOOL NAME TYPE	YOUR EFFECTIVENESS LEVEL (0-5)	YOUR ENJOYMENT LEVEL (0-5)
Wonderland School/ High Poverty Low Performing	5	2

NEGOTIATING YOUR SALARY

As a woman, you deserve to earn a fair and competitive salary. If you work in education, don't let anyone tell you that you can't negotiate your salary. Many times, people don't receive because they don't ask. In my situation with my first principalship, which came with a below average salary, I was able to negotiate a higher salary that I was comfortable with. I simply asked if there was any way to change my contract. The board required me to justify my request for a change in the set salary schedule. Previously, they hadn't had anyone to ask, but the board approved the salary changed due to the fact that I was accepting the principalship for their lowest performing school. The additional work that I would need to do to turn the school around was cited as the reason. You can do the same. If you are not satisfied with the offer, decline it!

You will save yourself some frustration and disappointment in the end. Don't settle for anything less than what you are worth!

FINAL TAKEAWAYS AND TIPS:

As women, we are responsible for many things, and we have to make a wise decision when we select where we will work. As a leader, your reputation can be put on the line and make it difficult for you to compete for jobs. 24. 1% of superintendents are women leaving men to make up 75. 9% of the superintendent positions in educational leadership.[3] As a woman, you can't afford to have a poor job performance evaluation because you accepted the wrong position. This could cause you to miss the job promotion. You want to be in the best position to excel and avoid having others say that you couldn't lead because you are a woman.

You have to make a decision based on what you want and what is available. I recommend rating the alignment between you and your potential employer. Determine if the information you gathered will make a good career fit. Don't be afraid to resend or decline an application or offer if you know that it's not the right fit for you.

---

3   "Boys Will Be Superintendents: School Leadership as a Gendered Profession ." Kappanonline.org, 3 Oct. 2018, www.kappanonline.org/maranto-carroll-cheng-teodoro-school-leadership-gender/

Reflective Questions
FOR READERS:

1. Why do you want to lead as the principal?

_____
_____
_____
_____
_____
_____
_____

2. Are you and your position (or desired position) the right fit? Why or why not?

_____
_____
_____
_____
_____
_____
_____
_____
_____
_____
_____

Chapter 6:
GIRL CODE:

TAKING CARE OF OTHER WOMEN IN LEADERSHIP

*T*HE FIRST DAY, after being appointed as principal, my instructional coach spoke these words to me:

> *Good afternoon, Ms. Riley, Thank you for taking the time to meet with me today to introduce yourself and to explain what you want to see done at School X. I look forward to working with you this year. I also wanted to tell you that I never wanted to be an administratrator until I met with you today. I look forward to learning from you.*

I was taken aback by what had been expressed, and I wondered about her past exposure to female principals. She and I had a very short meeting, and in that short amount of time, something that I did or said influenced her decision on administration. During our time working together, I was able to share some small nuggets of information about my role. I took her on as my mentee. By doing this, I felt that my coaching void would be fulfilled, and I would be helping a potential leader. This coaching experience would also be helpful in making me a better leader. I had someone who would be looking to me for leadership. Great principals were often great teachers. If you had built strong relationships with your students, it's a no brainer that you will find yourself building relationships with your staff members.

SOMEONE HELPED ME:

I feel a responsibility to help others, (um hello, I'm an educator). Because of this, I help others in every capacity of my educational career. During my educational trajectory, I received help and mentorship; therefore, I am passionate about helping others. As a teacher in my early twenties, I can recall the way the veteran teachers imparted knowledge to me on how to navigate as a first year teacher. These were my former teachers; they were eager to help me, and their help started on my first day on the job. These women had a real love for their profession, and they felt an obligation to cultivate the next generation of teachers. I will never forgot the support and love they showed to me.

When I became interested in the principalship, I had the privilege of having an highly effective principal, who served as my mentor. She allowed me to shadow her, complete my internship, and she gave me my first teacher leadership experience.

She changed my view on administration, and I was encouraged to know more about being a female principal. I wanted to learn how women could be empowered. I listened to and learned the secrets of success from those who were experienced and effective. My mentor shared the ways in which other female school leaders had uplifted her in the administration journey, and it was obvious in her role as a mentor.

WHAT IS THE GIRL CODE?

The Girl Code is the commitment to develop females by opportunity and uplift them as a form of women's empowerment. When operating under The Girl Code, females function in a safe space to ask questions, make mistakes, as well as have the freedom to grow. Leaders, who subscribe to this leadership mindset, are focused on developing female leaders with an idea of leadership legacy building. Women model expected leadership qualities for others, and they provide a positive and productive work environment where women are challenged and positioned for professional growth. Women empowerment is very important in our current society, based on gender equity. Empowerment occurs when women are committed to support each other and enable them to get some opportunities in different career fields.

There is a myth that women cannot work together due to jealousy, envy and holding grudges. This is untrue because women can work together, and they rarely judge each other. Some mistakes will be made as we face challenges and changes. Women are emotional beings, but this is what enables us to better understand each other and co-exist in harmony.

Let's dispel the myth that females can't work together. This is simply not true! Some of the greatest female organizations have been in existence for over one hundred years and are still going strong. Look at the history of the Girl Scouts of America which was organized in 1912 and Delta Sigma Theta Sorority, Incorporated which was organized in 1913. Both organizations have a primary focus on sisterhood and leveraging leadership to improve the global community.

RESPECTING THE GIRL CODE

Girl code should be respected and followed to the letter as it is everything a woman has.

It is very saddening to hear women say that they lack a female mentor, or they have never seen a female principal. Some might say that their principal is not approachable. The principalship is like a selective group. Many have the desire, but only a few are actively selected. Females make up 66% of elementary principals, but in secondary schools, females make up just 48% of principals in the the United States.[4] In order to see that number increase, we have to do a better job of nurturing and cultivating up-and-coming female principals. Respect the girl code by working together to create opportunities for women to be successful in leadership.

---

4   "Boys Will Be Superintendents: School Leadership as a Gendered Profession ." Kappanonline.org, 3 Oct. 2018, www.kappanonline.org/maranto-carroll-cheng-teodoro-school-leadership-gender/

KATRINA RILEY

IMPLEMENTATION OF THE GIRL CODE

MENTORSHIP

Women, who have achieved their dreams of school leadership should work in developing fellow women by guiding and encouraging them. They should act as role models to the younger generation. When administrators serve as role models, they can become better administrators and develop new skills. Learning and growing form a continuous process. When women build and strengthen each other, they are able to lead in many areas of school leadership, and they can have a positive impact on the communities they serve as they are able to collectively voice their needs from a united perspective. .

MOTIVATION: WOMEN MOTIVATING EACH OTHER

The principalship is hard work, but it can also be rewording work. During the challenging times in the role, motivation can make a big difference in our perspective of the work and help to encourage us to continue our work. Through motivation, one is able to carry on even when things seem to be difficult. Women should regularly motivate each other in everything that they purpose to do to avoid giving up. Nothing comes easy, and motivation is what makes us try new things as we get support from different people in life. Motivation leads to the realization of many dreams and pursuits in different careers, even the ones that are seen as jobs for men. Through motivation, a lot of women have made it in educational leadership roles because they had someone who cared enough to share their time to motivate them. With support, you can do things that seemed to be impossible.

BEING PASSIONATE ABOUT YOUR CAREER AND SHARING WITH OTHERS

Remember when you are working, there is always a person who is watching. The way you work can influence a person positively or negatively. As women, we should work with passion and vigor so that we can positively impact the people around us. The passion we show will make the younger women admire our work and focus on being better. We hope this will lead to a larger number of women choosing the administration field. When you are a passionate, female principal, the students that you lead will show interest in your work, and they can be encouraged to become principals. Being influential is a boost to our self-esteem, and it gives us a sense of pride.

VOLUNTEERING

NETWORKING BUILDING RELATIONSHIPS

Women should be encouraged to join some empowerment programs in order to succeed and have an impact in the state. When women are united, they become very powerful as they can speak in one voice. Women also have the opportunity through various organizations to reach young girls and aid in their development. Volunteering provides an opportunity for young girls to be empowered with the skills to become influential people in the future. They also gain some leadership qualities which are very vital in leadership. By sharing some ideas, women's groups also enhance some growth. Women are also able to set common goals and objectives which they aim to achieve after a period of time. In the modern world, a woman is a very important person. This is the reason why women should come together, uplift each other and provide a helping hand. As women, we should unite in order to achieve great things and change the world.

TIPS

1. If you don't have a positive story of female influencers and mentors along your path to the principalship, I encourage you to be different. Be the person that people can recognize as the one who helped them to be better.
2. Seek female mentors and build networks of other female leaders.
3. Volunteer your time and expertise to other aspiring female leaders to build a legacy.

FOR READERS

1. How can you begin to connect with other female school leaders in your area?

2. What professional organizations can you join to help mentor females aspiring to be school leaders?

Chapter 7:

OWN YOUR FEELINGS

OWNING YOUR FEELINGS

Do any of these statements sound familiar?

- I yelled at my staff today! Well, I didn't really yell, but I was upset, and I called an emergency meeting.
- I had a 'come to Jesus' meeting with my staff today. I was so angry! I could have cried.
- I get so upset, I just…"

We all have emotions, and that doesn't change because we become the principal. Females are born with more emotion than men. They have a hard time controlling emotions if they under a constant state of stress. However, how can we control the emotions we were destined to have, regardless of the situation? How can we use our emotions during work hours as a tool, instead of a hindrance? This chapter is devoted to help you handle your emotions as a female principal.

Keeping a check on your emotions while in places such as schools or in places of learning is a huge factor in today's society. If female leaders, like principals, lash out with emotions within the school environments, it could not only be catastrophic, it can have a long lasting effect on those trying to be a part of the educational process.

As a principal, I recall a day when I had to really check my feelings and hold my tears. During afternoon dismissal, my staff member began having a stroke in the middle of transition. I was the only adult standing near her when she began to fall backwards before eventually hitting her head on solid concrete. I had several student leaders working with transitions, and two classes had begun dismissal with their teachers. At the time, we had parents and buses waiting for students to be released. I had to place the school on immediate shutdown for emergency personnel to arrive. As I was kneeling with the staff member and yelling for assistance, I was terrified. I was afraid for my staff member, and I saw the fear and confusion from the students who had witnessed an adult fall. Once others began assisting the staff member, I went to reassure the students that the staff member was going to be okay. I felt my emotions rising, and I heard my voice begin to crack. I was quick to end my speech to the students, and I rushed to my office. I was unable to control my emotions. When I reached the door of my office, I was ready to feel a release from the heightened adrenaline and emotions of what had just happened. Once I opened the door, four student assistants who had been sent to my office during the lockdown, were staring right at me. No crying was allowed just yet as they were looking for reassurance and answers. Eventually, I was able to cry in my car, as I pulled out of the parking lot of the school.

    Female principals have to take notice of their emotions on a second by second basis. It is highly important for this particular job because of the environment. The environment is a learning environment, and if female principals are allowed to rage, cry or even show too many of their emotions, those that are in the learning mindset will only think that it is acceptable to do the same. Being too emotional, is not acceptable for growing minds, and it is unprofessional for the doer. It is important to be our true, authentic self, even as a principal leader. People can tell if we are not being who we really are. Parents, the community, students, and staff are in need of a leader who has the strength to lead during an emergency. You were hired based on who YOU are. All the groups that are in need of leadership will require and expect different things from you; however, you must always recognize the woman in the mirror. I recommend that you really get in touch with who you are, what you stand for, and what you believe in. We, as female leaders, need to teach others by showing action, and if action consists of an unbalanced emotion, then that action will only be heightened by those that are around the instability. In addition, you must get in check with your feelings and emotions.

    As a principal, you will have a range of emotions that comes along with the tremendous amount of work that you will be required to do. You may be angry in faculty meetings, sad after the benchmark scores are released, and overjoyed when your school receives positive accolades. In all those moments, you are the leader and have a team of people who are expecting you to be a leader with enduring strength. In education, there are exciting and happy moments of discovery in which we relish. Moments of extreme disappointment and despair can cripple us. Both moments can bring emotions and often tears. As a principal, is it okay to share those moments publicly? All women will cry; however, all women will not cry all the time. Is it socially acceptable for a woman to cry? It is socially acceptable for the female principal to cry?

There are numerous ways to control our emotions, or even use them as a tool for teaching. If the proper use of emotion is utilized for problem solving and motivation, then those that are being taught will understand how they can use emotions to their benefits as well. If you follow these few guidelines, you will have success in your workplace.

FIRST: OWN YOUR FEELINGS!

If you understand that females are emotional creatures, it is good to stay in touch with your emotions. Suppressing them is not a good ideal. You are not widget; you are human, and humans have feelings. Moreover, you are also a leader and a professional. You lead by example and model the expected behavior of others. As a professional, you must own your feelings and hold yourself accountable for your actions. You cannot lead and blame others for your reactions to your emotions and feelings. Understand that it is natural to have emotions; however, it is not emotionally healthy to suppress them. Take ownership of those emotions, identify them and practice effective coping skills. If you keep your emotions bottled-up, then they are bound to come out at a most inopportune time.

If you are thinking that you are just sitting behind a computer, or if you are thinking of how to create a solution to a problem, be aware that your emotions are involved. An emotion is not a part of a detached reality; in fact, it is an important function of our physical beings. If you fail to deal with negative emotions, you can cause long term damage on your brain. You can also form habits that will allow you to express yourself in ways that are inconceivable. Do not suppress your emotions; own your feelings and find the ability to use an outlet when negative emotions arise. You can use breathing as a technique to relax, or you can write your thoughts in a small journal. After the emotion subsides, reassess the situation.

SECOND: KEEP COMPOSURE AND COMPARTMENTALIZE EMOTIONS

If you understand the ability of mastering yourself and owning your feelings, you will want to keep your composure, and compartmentalize the emotions. As principals, we need to have a heightened understanding of this strategy because there are so many stressors that come with the job. While at work, we need to be aware and in control at all times. Sometimes, that can be hard to do when certain situations occur.

If principals have the ability to teach and change the face of education, then they need to teach themselves to master and compartmentalize their own thoughts before proceeding with any sharing of information. As you lead by example, it will be helpful for the principal to model composure and control before the students and coworkers. Modeling leadership, by example, will send a powerful message to those you lead.

THIRD: FOLLOW THE TIP GUIDE BELOW

To control your emotions in the workplace and notice a huge change in you, and with others that you are around, follow some specific tips. Before you walk into your workplace, there are a few key aspects to be considered to help you reevaluate your emotions. Alternatively, they can be a guide to help you during a situation when you feel your emotions arise. In fact, you will be able to help others and teach them these tips.

TIPS:

FIX YOUR FACE:

How to fix your face in meetings: You do not want the world to know what you are thinking, especially when you think that you have just heard the most ridiculous comment. People are constantly watching you and your reactions. Tips that I have used, and still use today, are internal conversations and self-talk. First, smile, to show the direct opposite facial expression of what you are thinking. Next, say to yourself, "I'm smiling because this is so dumb, and I just have to smile." Count to ten while you are smiling. At this time, your mind and body are scrambling, and you have temporarily checked out of the moment. Physically, you look like you are still there.

LEAVE PERSONAL MATTERS AT HOME.

Bringing them with you can cause negativity instead or productivity. This also includes talking about personal matters. Talking and bringing personal matters into the workplace can be like a plague, once it is started, then others will think it is alright to say and act the same. By the end of the meeting, you would have only brought a cloud of negativity that will continue to expand.

BREATHE AND RELAX.

Breathing techniques have been proven to lower emotions and allow the user to calmly address the situation before it gets out of hand.

USE THE 10-SECOND RULE.

As a child, everyone learned this technique, and it actually works with adults. Take a deep breath and count to ten.

CLARIFY THE SITUATION.

It is easier to clarify the situation at hand. In the beginning, it could have been something as simple as a miscommunication; therefore, do not react too quickly. Calmly address every part of the situation before continuing to solve it.

ALLOW OTHERS TO SPEAK.

Allow others to speak and let them get their point of view out before you speak. You are a leader, allow them to express their feelings first. When they see how calm you are when you respond, then they will naturally begin to calm down. If you start to push them for answers that you are not getting, they will start to lash out in the opposite direction. Stay calm and allow them to say what they need to say first. Show them how quality leadership is effective.

CONTROL TRIGGERS.

If you know that you are angry, then know how to control your triggers. Anticipate what is going to happen in the situation, analyze it and respond accordingly and professionally. Teachers and principals, who use this technique within their educational environments, are highly successful with mastering their emotions.

NOTE TAKING.

Always having something to capture notes will allow you to use this tip. I begin by simply writing anything so that I am not driven by my emotions or allowing others to see what I am thinking.

DO NOT CRY.

As for crying, my general rule is to try your best not to cry publicly about any of the following situations: Poor test scores, frustration, pushed back on ideas, disagreements, rude comments, stressful situations, or in front of students. Crying at work can show a weakness, and it can reveal that you are not a master of your craft. Wait until you are at home or go and take a few minutes to relax. Do not allow others to see you cry, and you will need to stay controlled for those around you. A good leader will put those emotions on hold until the proper time to let them out.

As a leader, you publicly put your best self out front. You are also the one who motivates others to believe in your vision and push themselves to do more in spite of obstacles.

However, there are moments when crying can be acceptable.

Crying might be acceptable during joyous moments, or while listening to a touching story. In these moments you will show a sense of vulnerability that can be appreciated by your staff.

LASTLY, EXERCISE.

By the end of the day, if you still feel a rise in your emotions, wait until you get home and go for a run. Exercise only helps us to release the extra buildup that we all get on a daily basis, and it helps to calm your mind. It is almost like sweating the negativity out. If you do a run or workout in the morning before work, it has been known to lower emotional outbursts for the rest of the day. It helps you stay healthy and look great.

TIPS AND TAKEAWAYS.

Since you are a female principal, it is wise to know how to master your emotions and own your feelings. It is always good to know the triggers that prompt you to get emotional. If you can keep your emotions in check while at work, then you can lead by example and show others why you are a great leader. They will automatically know that you have full composure, and they will respond and learn faster. Just remember to stay calm and reassess the situations before you react. If you are still angry at the end of the day, push that emotion out with exercise. All females principals can learn to have more control over their emotions. It just takes time to understand that the emotion is not what leads to results. Proper action and quality leadership will provide results.

FOR READERS

1. What techniques can you use to control your emotions?

2. As a principal, what are some experiences that will make you cry?

Chapter 8:
SUPERGIRL: EFFECTIVE DELEGATION FOR GETTING IT ALL DONE

*I*WAS NOTIFIED OF my first principal assignment five days prior to teachers returning from summer break. At the time of notification, I was living approximately two hours away from the school. I had not secured housing or packed a single box in preparation for the move. Additionally, I didn't have a secretary, bookkeeper, or assistant principal who had been hired. Prior to becoming a principal, doing everything myself was common. As an assistant principal, it was uncommon to have someone dedicated to assist you in that role. Often times, I would work with a team of other assistant principals to bounce ideas around; however, delegation of tasks was was not something that I could do at that level. Naturally, I wasn't very skilled at allowing someone to help me; therefore, I quickly recognized that delegation was a weakness of mine. With having such little time to get incubated to the the new school, I had to quickly learn how to delegate and how to delegate well.

You can't really do it all , but you are responsible for it all. As a principal, you are ultimately responsible for everything in your building. You are expected to be in the know of the daily operations, the budget and instruction. You should be aware of everything that is going on in your building. A mentor once shared that principals don't get enough credit for things that go right, but they get all the credit for the things that go wrong. Because of this, you are responsible for it all; however, you can not do it all. This may sound odd and for some, this may be extremely difficult to conceive, but you can not do everything. Unfortunately, as women. we are not walking around with a magic cape with a large S on the back that allows us to be in multiple places at the same time, have xray vision to see what is happening behind closed doors or even scale tall buildings. No super cape is given to you at the time of hire to assist you with running an effective school building. Most women still have additional obligations outside of their role as principal, such as church and civic duties, family obligations, and personal interests. Imagine what would happen if you did all the tasks that you are responsible for, in addition to the outside obligations, all by yourself. You would not last very long, and you would eventually hit burn out, as discussed in another chapter. The most difficult thing to do, as a female principal, is to discard the imaginary cape and seek assistance. You are strong; you are independent, but you are not wearing a super cape. You must do something to to help yourself be Super.

LEARN TO DELEGATE:

Perhaps you have done everything by yourself for many years. As an assistant principal, you may not have had anyone to delegate to, or it was frowned upon. In either case, not delegating has become a habit for you. For the sake of your sanity, that practice must be broken. For some, delegating is difficult. Is is because we want to be liked by others? Is it because we want to appear strong and independent? Are you fearful that others will perceive us or accuse us of being lazy? Will we be accused of being a DIVA? Are we fearful that the results may not be what we are expecting? The reasons for these fears are often a part of our internal thoughts, and we can't allow them to become reality. Overcoming this mindset and resistance to delegation is the beginning of building a relationships with people.

THE IMPORTANCE OF DELEGATING:

Delegating is important because it provides balance in your work, and it also helps you to build capacity in your building. In addition, delegating builds trust among teams which leads to loyalty which aids in your efforts to galvanize teams. There is brain research to suggest that when people feel trusted they produce more oxytocin in the brain.[5] The more this chemical is produced,

---

5   Kosfeld, M, et al. "Oxytocin Increases Trust in Humans." *Current Neurology and Neuroscience Reports.* , U. S. National Library of Medicine, 2 June 2005, www.ncbi. nlm. nih. gov/pubmed/15931222.

the more trustworthy they become, and trust can be given in return. Overall, delegating should become a strength among teams and one strength that female leaders must develop to be successful. As a general rule delegating should do the following:

- Build accountability
- Build capacity
- Build a stronger team

HOW TO DELEGATE:

For many principals and school leaders, it is difficult to let go and delegate an important task to others and trust that it is completed in the manner that you wish. For others, they may delegate to others, but they spend so much time worrying if the task will be completed. They fail to focus on other important duties. We have a group called micro managers who delegate, but they pester those who have been given assignments. In order to delegate well, you must delegate to people you trust, set clear expectations, and set checkpoints to monitor the progress.

DELEGATE TO PEOPLE YOU TRUST

As mentioned earlier, delegation builds trust in others; however, it is important to delegate to people whom you trust to complete the tasks. In order to do that, you must be mindful of the skillset of your team members and be willing to see the potential growth in them. Identity employees who express passion and have a desire and a particular interest. Review certification areas and expertise from past work experiences, and then give team members an opportunity to show their capabilities. It is important to know your own strengths and weaknesses and have individuals who can support you in them. This can save time for you because learning new skills take time and with district and state demands, time is something we don't have. It is smart to delegate to others. If you have tasks that require skills that you are deficient in, delegate these tasks to someone who has strong skills in that area.

SET CLEAR EXPECTATIONS

Good leaders set clear expectations, and setting clear expectations is key to being a solid delegator. Take the time to explain what your expectations are for completing the tasks. This will help to build a solid understanding of your expectations as a leader for others to follow. As a school leader, your time is valuable, and taking time to set your expectations early will allow you to save time for giving additional information, answering and clarifying questions.

SET CHECKPOINTS TO MONITOR PROGRESS

You don't want people to feel as if they have wasted valuable time completing an assigned project incorrectly. This frustrates the person to whom you have delegated to do a task, and it wastes valuable time that could have been more effectively used for other assignments. To avoid this, I recommend building set check ins to figure out status updates and to ensure that the projects seem to be in line with your expectations. During your check ins, you can give directions and assistance if the person is misguided or seems to be misundersing the expected outcomes. To avoid confusion, let people know, in advance, when you will be checking in and what they should have available for the check ins.

RECOGNIZE THAT PEOPLE WILL MAKE MISTAKES

Everyone, including you, will make mistakes. Save yourself additional frustration by realizing and accepting this fact. How you handle the mistakes while delegating to others is what matters. Each interaction with staff is an opportunity to build and maintain trust. Build a trusting, working relationship by making it safe for people who might make mistakes. If a team member has misunderstood a delegated task, use tact in guiding them in making corrections. Instead of jumping to conclusions and holding on to the mistakes, embrace the mistakes as an opportunity for growth and development. Redirect with clear expectations and reset checkpoints.

DELEGATING TIPS:

Make yourself the first manager- When you become the principal, you must keep repeating to yourself that you are the leader. You run the show, and you call the shots. No one manages this environment more than you do. I have seen many people who abuse the power of delegating. Yes, this is a reality. You have to make sure that you are managing the things in your building.

DELEGATE VS PASSING THE BUCK

As an assistant principal, I hated bus duty. When I became a principal, I promised myself that I would assign bus duty to someone else. When school started, I did just that. I assigned the busy duty to my assistant principal. What I didn't know at that time was that the car rider area was the largest population of students; therefore, I had given myself the heaviest task. I was assigned for duty in the car rider area. I hated the bus loading zone for various reasons. As the principal, I couldn't just assign that task and completely walk away. I would visit the area and make sure that the procedures were in place and running smoothly, and I would get updates from the assistant principal on duty during our meetings. Some days, we would take turns being in different areas to exchange feedback on ways to improve. I showed an interest in one of the duties I disliked, and I stayed connected to the process.

SHARED LEADERSHIP:

As the leader of the building, there are multiple times when you will need to delegate certain parts of a project to other people in a shared leadership role. Shared leadership roles are opportunities for someone else, along with you, to be responsible for completing tasks. When I was a principal, my assistant principal and I had many shared leadership roles. It allowed me to delegate while giving her additional leadership experiences to develop her skills

DELEGATION CHART

TASK	DELEGATE	DO NOT DELEGATE	SHARED LEADERSHIP
Assignment from superintendent		X	
community member needs information regarding the status of the school		X	
secretarial tasks, writing memos, draft emails	X		
Schedules, reports, record keeping	X		
Discipline Referrals	X		
Ordering Materials	X		
Curriculum			X
Assessments*	X (managing state materials)		X

TIPS:

- Delegate to people you trust.
- Don't' be completely hands off when you delegate tasks, stay connected.
- Remember, you are the face of the school, and your reputation becomes the reputation of the school. Don't delegate tasks when you can't control the narrative.

Reflective Questions
FOR READERS:

1. What fears do you have about delegating tasks to others?

_____
_____
_____
_____
_____
_____
_____
_____

2. Who are individuals you trust? Why?

_____
_____
_____
_____
_____
_____

3. Who are individuals that can grow from being responsible for a delegated task?

4. What tasks can you begin delegating today?

Chapter 9: TOP MISTAKES FEMALE PRINCIPALS MAKE AND HOW TO AVOID THEM

BECOMING A PRINCIPAL is an immense and enormous deal. People have several perceptions of you, as a female principal, that differ from those they have of male principals. Skilled female leaders are proof of resolute, determination and effort. Nonetheless, there are obstacles to being a female leader. Mistakes in the role are common and to be expected. You can poll principals in any phase of their principalship, and you can be sure to find that mistakes have been made along the way. I've made countless mistakes, as a principal, and have been fortunate enough to learn from each of them. I've forgotten to approve payroll before a vacation; I've deleted the wrong email and documents, and I've omitted red beans and rice off the menu for a staff luncheon—a big no no in Louisiana. I got desperate and hired a poor teacher. This is just a short list of the many mistakes that I've made as a principal. One thing that I learned during all of my mistakes was that it was important to learn and grow from them in order to not allow that same mistake to happen again. By doing this, I grew stronger in creating and implementing systems, and I became a more proactive thinker . After speaking with other principals, I learned how common it was for principals to make mistakes. After all, we are human. In order to help build and train our upcoming legacy for female principals, it is important to share the most common mistakes that female principals make. It is important for us to share this information with each other and those who are anticipating choosing educational leadership as a career. Below are top errors female principals make and how to evade them:

1. ACCEPTING THE WRONG POSITION.

When people are eager to be promoted to the next level, often times there is little focus given to the potential employer. In some cases, the applicant has a general knowledge of the organization or the employer but not enough to check for really important things that can determine alignment.

    Many times, I was attracted to a job because of the salary, or the title, and I knew very little information about the place that I would spend most of my time. In fact, almost all of my jobs I've had as a leader started with the same limited information.

Here are some things you want to know about your potential employer BEFORE you accept a job: Note: you want to make sure that you are gathering information about the organization (district, charter, non profit, etc.) as well as your supervisor (boss, superintendent, director, etc.)

- Values that drive their work
- Employment patterns
- Expectations for completing the work
- Current work culture

2. NOT UNDERSTANDING THE HISTORICAL/ CULTURAL NARRATIVE

The first thing you should do is a background accumulation. Knowing the historical background of the school is important. Knowing with whom you will intersect at the onset of your employment matters. The kind of people you should seek from the beginning should include the historian who will know where the bones, history of the school, are buried, The historian can tell you what has gone on in the past history of the building. It's important to know this information in order to avoid the mistake of not respecting school traditions and other historical symbolism. You want to find out what has been happening in the building. The historian may be your veteran teacher, a bookkeeper, a custodian, or even the assistant principal. In order to cope with the school culture, it is necessary to know some historical facts to discern the traditions that need to be retained. Make sure you meet with the right people to gather the right information that you will need.

3. BEING UNAPPROACHABLE

For staff to want to approach you with ideas, suggestions and concerns, you have to appear approachable, which may make you feel a bit vulnerable. Let people know who you are. Even in the age of social media, your employees want to know who their boss is. You want to build professional work relationships with your staff to build trust and loyalty. Permit people to recognize your personality. Considering we are in a digitalized era, managers and employees need to be aware of the kind of person you are. You should desire to set up professional work correlations with your staff members. If they cannot understand you, chances are, they will certainly not like you. Make sure the office door is open and always reassure your presence. You can also set meetings in which you get feedback from the members. This will give insight into what is currently happening in the school, and it will also help you diagnose problems before they arise. An informal chit chat with staff members, or pitching in to help with school projects can really go a long way in building the rapport you need for the staff to come to you with anything concerning the school.

4. NOT SETTING CLEAR EXPECTATIONS

Make sure you unfold to others what you are planning and outline your ambitions from the start. This imparts focus, assists you in measuring your progress, gives you motivation and also allows you to systemize your time and resources to make the most out of them. Setting clear expectations can help you build trust by displaying adequacy or effectiveness.

5. NOT HAVING BUILT A SUPPORT TEAM

Working solely, or as an island, can make your work difficult. Devise your leadership crew and effectively disperse leadership. The aim of a team is to win. Teamwork encourages creativity and healthy risk-taking, and it builds trust, and it teaches skills in conflict resolution. Members, on a team, may possess unique strengths that can be incorporated in the workplace to enhance performance. When you work as a team, you will accomplish great things. Implement distributive leadership within your building by assigning specific responsibilities to team members and hold each member accountable for the area and the overall success of the school. Here is a sample of a distributive leadership form:

DISTRIBUTED LEADERSHIP

ADMINISTRATIVE LEADER	AREAS OF RESPONSIBILITY	DUTIES
PRINCIPAL	• Provide a safe and secure environment that promotes academic and social success. • Lead and Coordinate all instructional programs. • Welcome a diverse population of students and staff while providing the necessary support to ensure their success. • Establish, foster, and sustain a healthy relationship with the community. • Manage and coordinate facility upkeep and operations to ensure an environment conducive to the highest level of learning. • Identify, hire and retain highly qualified experienced staff through meaningful professional development and ethical practices. • Ensure overall school vision, functions, and operations are aligned with district policies, initiatives and programs along with compliance with state and federal statutes.	• Instruction-Secondary • Title 1 • ESE • Leadership/SDM • PTO/SAC • Academic Support • School Messenger • Facilities/Events • Duty (am, pm, lunch)

ASSISTANT PRINCIPAL

- Assist with providing a safe and secure environment that promotes academic and social success and welcomes a diverse population of students and staff.
- Assist with leading and coordinating all instructional programs.
- Assist with managing and coordinating facility upkeep and operations to ensure an environment conducive to the highest level of learning.
- Assist with establishing, fostering, and sustaining a healthy relationship with the community.
- Assist with identifying, hiring, and retaining highly qualified experienced staff through meaningful professional development and ethical practices.
- Provide assistance with ensuring the overall school vision, functions, and operations are aligned with district policies, initiatives and programs along with compliance with state and federal statutes.
- Manage and progress monitor student social growth and development.
- Coordinate and facilitate testing operations and implementation.

- Instruction-Primary
- Title 1
- Guidance
- Busses
- Textbooks
- Testing
- Facilities/Events
- Newsletter
- Team up
- Enrichment
- Marquee
- PTO/SAC
- New Teacher Induction
- Discipline
- Duty (am, pm, lunch)

DEAN

- Provide daily Behavioral Support within classrooms
- Serve as direct school liaison for all Behavioral Support teachers/paraprofessionals with district support staff.
- Participate in relevant school-based Multidisciplinary Team (MT) Meetings, SMARTeam meetings, and any other meetings relevant to students served in Behavioral Support classrooms.
- Monitor, model and assist with the implementation of academic instruction and social skills curriculum.
- Assist in the development of appropriate IEP goals, objectives and data collection system.
- Provide crisis intervention counseling when students are in crisis.
- Assist teachers with creating and maintaining a Portfolio (Parent/Guardian/Surrogate contact information, IEP, FBA/PBIP, copies of point sheets, anecdotal logs, discipline referrals, parent contact log) for each student.

DISTRIBUTED LEADERSHIP

ADMINISTRATIVE LEADER	AREAS OF RESPONSIBILITY
READING COACH	- Coordinate and facilitate ongoing professional development in Reading that aligns to student and teacher needs. - Compose and distribute the expectations for the classroom environment. - Support teachers with planning and delivering lessons that align with student deficiencies. (modeling) - Provide instructional support aligned to teacher and student needs. (coaching) - Coordinate and facilitate school activities that encourage and support student success in Reading.
READING INTERVENTIONIST	- Remediate students that do not meet proficiency criteria in Reading. - Meet consistently with at-risk students. - Progress monitor non-proficient students. - Select and create curriculum to meet specific student needs.

MATH COACH	- Coordinate and facilitate ongoing professional development in Math that aligns to student and teacher needs. - Compose and distribute the expectations for the classroom environment. - Support teachers with planning and delivering lessons that align with student deficiencies. (modeling) - Provide instructional support aligned to teacher and student needs. (coaching) - Coordinate and facilitate school activities that encourage and support student success in Math.	
GUIDANCE COUNSELOR	- Provide and monitor RTI services for all identified students - Support students in developing peer relationships, effective social and decision making skills and conflict resolution strategies. - Assist with managing and monitoring student social growth and development. - Assist teachers in providing tier 2 and 3 behavior interventions. - Coordinate outreach services and community support services that align with the needs of students and staff.	- Safety Patrol Sponsor - Assist with student Attendance Meetings - MRT Meeting - RTI - Character Education - Student Crisis Responder

GUIDANCE COUNSELOR	• Provide individual counseling to students as needed. • Participate in school-based Multidisciplinary Team (MT) Meetings, SMARTeam meetings, and any other meetings relevant to students needs.	
SECURITY	• Assist with managing and monitoring student social growth and development. • Assist teachers in providing tier 2 and 3 behavior interventions. • Provide individual counseling to students as needed. • Provide safety interventions for the school	• ISSP

6. CONSTITUTING CHANGES RAPIDLY

This is a common mistake that many principals make. See to it that you expend some time monitoring the occurrence of things around the school before altering anything. Recall that comprehending the historical background is important. Abrupt changes may form uncertainties and vandalize your associations by causing mistrust. For the sake of retaining a good reputation and maintaining staff support, modify or change things only when you possess an exhaustive plan to reinstate it . It is also wise to gain input from staff members on certain matters. Contemplate the objectives, repercussions and how the change will influence others. Acknowledge safety issues, as well as any violations of laws, whether direct or indirect.

7. NOT ASKING FOR HELP

You can ask for help when you have a lot on your plate. Asking for assistance helps to build relationships with your colleagues and also drives in productivity. Construct a team of support that you trust. You can add the following to your team: professional colleagues that are experienced, and an unbiased expert, who can be a principal coach, who has adeptness in that field. Avoid novice colleagues as well as staff who lack brilliance. You can seek out this assistance from multiple sources, including principal groups and organizations, online membership organizations and your district. You can find these organizations online with a simple Google search. I recommend principalnerd.com and the Facebook group for administrators: www.facebook.com/principalnerdtribe.

8. HIRING LACK LUSTER STAFF

Great principals hire great teachers. The practice of hiring teachers, who are low performers, is the same as employing team wreckers. They rip the team apart and bring about the loss of tenability in the community at large. Dignified leaders should employ outstanding teachers they can be proud of and those that can positively influence others. Employ with a perspective of that person who can carry out services, even when there is a budget setback.

Below are sample interview questions to help you identify staff worthy to be on your team:

- Why did you decide to become a teacher?
- Why do you want to teach at this school?
- What can you bring to our school that makes you unique?
- What frustrates you the most in a classroom?
- What is your teaching philosophy?
- How would you prepare your classroom if it were the first day of school?
- How do you evaluate students?
- Why do we teach "X" in school?
- How do you communicate with parents?
- What are your strengths and weaknesses as a teacher?

9. NOT TAKING TIME TO CELEBRATE STAFF

As a new principal, it is easy to find problems and want to fix them, however, not having a balance of criticism and praise can be problematic. The staff members morale is a significant factor that slips out of the minds of many principals. It may not necessarily be their fault since they are also involved in handling school issues. However, employees require inspiration to keep up with productivity. Make it a norm to celebrate staff members. As a principal, you can put in order staff motivation programs, such as monthly staff parties, outings, certificates for best performers and even door signs. These activities give the members a positive mentality towards working with you.

Keep in mind the natural swings in staff morale (see image below) and plan activities and events accordingly.

Examples of staff morale boosters:

- Notes of appreciation
- Pop UP Snack Cart
- Staff Potluck
- Seasonal Staff Surprises- Valentine treats, Staff Trick or Treat

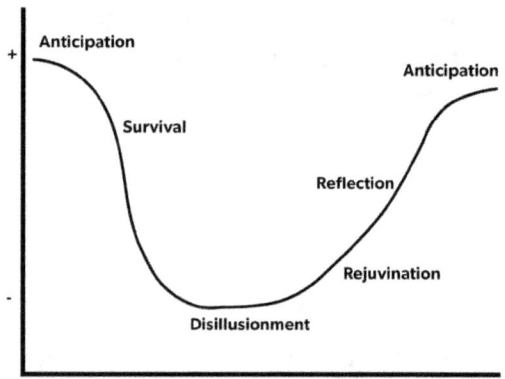

The Evolution of a Teacher by Dr. Mark Littleton and Dr. Pam Littleton." *The Evolution of a Teacher by Dr. Mark Littleton and Dr. Pam Littleton.* [6]

---

6   The Evolution of a Teacher by Dr. Mark Littleton and Dr. Pam Littleton." The Evolution of a Teacher by Dr. Mark Littleton and Dr. Pam Littleton.

10. NOT SETTING BOUNDARIES; BEING TOO PERSONAL

A "comfy" relationship with one staff or board member may induce a feeling to the other members that they are being left out or they may consider the behavior as tapering off. Make sure the associations with colleagues and members of the staff are healthy. Carry out random acts of kindness without being biased. You should also monitor your social media. I highly recommend that you should adjust your privacy settings to avoid your staff from having too much knowledge about your after school activities. You will want to control the perception that one may have about you, as well as have a healthy dose of professional distance. Change your settings to avoid having unpleasant posts added to your timeline or images of you tagged without your permission.

FINAL TAKEAWAYS & TIPS

As a female principal, anticipate that mistakes will happen. Accept the mistakes and take responsibility for your mishap. Your mistakes can be an opportunity to learn and grow if you take the time to reflect and review the process. Ask yourself questions about what went wrong and how a different outcome could have been achieved. Don't lose your focus or derail your progress because of a mistake. Take a moment to process your responses and learn to rebound, quickly. As a leader, how you respond to your mistakes will model the process for aspiring school principals. You will show your followers how to be a resilient leader. As a principal, do a self-evaluation and use the results for self- improvement.

FOR READERS:

1. How have you handled mistakes in the past?

_____
_____
_____
_____
_____
_____
_____
_____
_____
_____

2. How do you plan to avoid the top mistakes female principals make?

_____
_____
_____
_____
_____

Chapter 10:

NEW PRINCIPAL 101

*B*EING A NEW principal is exciting! You have been dreaming of having your own school and you have worked hard to prove that you are well-prepared for the job. Getting to the principal's seat is not an easy task, it will require countless hours of preparation. Before I got to the principal's seat, I had invested many hours in my preparation. When you become a new principal, spend a lot of time thinking about what you need to do going in the door. Mental preparation is a requirement for being an effective leader and in handling the leadership responsibilities of a principal. When you get to the door of your school, be prepared and confident in your new role as the leader. In the previous chapters of this book, the focus has been on self-care and preparation; however, this particular chapter is specifically tailored to new principles and what you need to do to be your best self as a new principal.

FIRST IMPRESSIONS:

Your first impressions are lasting impressions, especially as a new principal. Your actions will be judged from the moment you are hired. Your employees, parents and community will judge you on how and when you communicate with others, your attire, body language and when you don't speak. You will be constantly reviewed by your employees. What will be the staff's first impression of you? How will you introduce yourself? As a new principal, make the best impression by remembering to be confident, friendly, and to greet everyone. Typically, there will be an opportunity to tour/walk your campus for the first time. Depending on the time of hire, you may or may not have staff members inside your building. In any case, you are making first impressions to staff, students and any stakeholders with whom you may come into contact.

SOCIAL MEDIA MANAGEMENT

Social media can give your new staff a first impression of you even before they meet you in person. In the age of social media, it has become common to google someone, or take a look at someone's personal facebook page. Depending on your personal settings, you may be opened to any one taking a peek into your personal life. I recommend "dumping" your social media by changing your personal settings to limit what information is visible to others and allowing tags of pictures and posts to be approved before being added to your timeline. To take additional precautions, you can even, temporarily, change your profile name and pictures.

YOUR IMPRESSIONS OF THE CAMPUS, PEOPLE, AND STUDENTS

During your first initial school visit, you are also taking first impression notes on what you observe. Here is a list of what to look for:

Campus walks- with previous principal (if possible) or someone who has perspective of the building.

- What to look for when school is in session
- Classroom setups
- What students are doing
- What adults are doing
- Reading the room - what are the values being displayed?
- Pulse check of school- where is the liveliness?
- Student movement patterns (ie pick up, dismissal, class changes, lunch etc)
- Student common areas- any safety concerns?
- What are support staff doing? Where are they located?
- Your office
- Campus layout
- Identity any potential safety concerns
- Main office- how are adults interacting with others?

What was your first impression?
- What to look for when school is not in session
- Who is working?
- How does summer school cleaning session look? - can you determine a process? Who is responsible?
- Your office
- How the classrooms were left over the summer

Who are the people I need to meet? As a new principal, there will be many people who are going to want to schedule meetings with you. To keep your calendar prioritized, there are certain groups of people you should meet with immediately after your appointment.

WHO TO MEET WITH	WHEN TO MEET	PURPOSE/ QUESTIONS
PREVIOUS PRINCIPAL (IF APPLICABLE)	Within 1st week, prior to tour of school campus	Past information on the school, staff member information
SUPERVISOR	Within first 2 days of hire	How to hire/fire How to spend money Curriculum overview Expectations
TEACHERS	1st and 2nd week after tour of campus	Gathering information Hearing suggestions

ASSISTANT PRINCIPAL	Within first week	Background of the school Establishing expectations
SECRETARY	Week 1	Meet and Greet Setting expectations Scheduling appointments with community/board meetings and teacher meet and greets
BOOKKEEPER	Week 2	Meet and Greet Setting expectations
COMMUNITY/ BOARD MEMBERS	Week 3	Building relationships Sharing vision

BUDGET AND FINANCE—WHAT YOU SHOULD KNOW AS A NEW PRINCIPAL

Most aspiring principals will say that budget is one of the areas in which they always want more training. Each school district has different rules on budget proceedings, however, here are some basic information for new principals.

- Request an audit and most recent audit records
- Determine any outstanding amounts
- Determine what materials have been ordered for the upcoming school year
- Identify deposit schedule for the upcoming year

- Update signature cards

GET ORGANIZED:

Make sure that you put systems in place to help you to be organized and effective. Simple things can help you stay on top of important tasks and items.

PAPERWORK:

- Note keeping tool: (Section small notebook- section 1 for any notes from your supervisor or info about the school you are capturing, section 2 for Meetings, or trainings you attend section 3 for any running list of ideas and checklist items)
- Keep a Journal: begin to keep a journal to capture your excitement and rewarding events as a first year principal. At any time, look back over your journal.

CALENDAR:

- Highlight section for long hours and recurring events.
- Set reminders
- Try electronic calendars. (Outlook, Google)

THE FOLLOWING PAGES ARE SAMPLE TEMPLATES THAT NEW PRINCIPALS CAN USE

SAMPLE WELCOME LETTER FOR PARENTS

Happy Land School
2854 Happy Street
Happy City, Happy State
Telephone (xxx) 123-3122 • Fax (xxx) 123-3122
YOU, Principal

Dear Parents/Guardians:

We are excited that you have chosen SCHOOL NAME. The first day of school for students is Date. My name is NAME, and I would like to take this opportunity to introduce myself as the Principal of SCHOOL NAME. I am very excited to begin this wonderful school year, full of wonderful changes! My educational belief is that all children deserve a quality education and that all children can achieve at high levels. At SCHOOL NAME we value:

Respect, Leadership, Scholarship

My vision for the school is: To improve the educational opportunities, preparation, and academic results for all children at SCHOOL NAME. Our goal is to provide our scholars with the best education in a safe learning environment. At SCHOOL NAME, scholars will participate in a comprehensive curriculum, which emphasizes reading, writing, problem solving, and have any early exposure to leadership skills that will increase their college and career readiness. Please take a moment to review some important reminders below:

SAMPLE WELCOME LETTER FOR PARENTS

Registration Guidelines
(Photo ID required and 2 proofs of residency from the list below.): ADD YOUR INFORMATION BELOW

- All new students MUST register using the new district registration criteria (no exceptions)
- All returning students MUST re-register using the new district registration criteria (no exceptions)

Proof of Address:

- Current water or electric bill
- Current phone bill
- Current mortgage
- Current lease agreement with leasing office contact information
- Current bank statement (please mark-out account numbers)
- Current payroll statement (please mark-out account numbers)
- Current auto insurance statement (please mark-out account numbers)

***Altered address information will NOT be accepted

SAMPLE WELCOME LETTER FOR PARENTS

School starts at 8:30 am and will end at 3:00 pm. To ensure adequate safety and supervision, please make sure your child does NOT arrive to school before 8:00 am. Students should arrive to school between 8:00 am and 8:20 am so they can eat breakfast. Pre-K students must be taken directly to their classroom by an adult, and during dismissal, they can only be picked up by an adult/daycare. Kindergarten, 1st, 2nd, 3rd, 4th, and 5th grade students will report directly to their classrooms on the first of school only. After that, they will report to the front of the school and sit on the benches.

All students (Prek-5th) will be required to wear school uniforms each day (Mon-Fri). Please take the time, now, to purchase your child's school uniforms. We have listed several businesses that carry school uniforms for an affordable price. Uniforms should be purchased slightly larger than your child's actual size to give him/her room to grow into their clothes throughout the year.

Throughout the school year, there will be opportunities for parent/guardian involvement via the Parent Teacher Association (PTA) and/or the School Advisory Council (SAC). Please join these two organizations and visit WEBSITE for more information regarding school and district activities.

The SCHOOL NAME family looks forward to working with you to ensure that your child is academically and socially prepared to meet grade level expectations for promotion and to ultimately become a productive member of society.

Sincerely,
NAME
TITLE

QUICK SCHOOL ASSESSMENT GUIDE

Quick School Assessment–Upon Enty/New Hire

POSSIBLE EVIDENCE SOURCES

- Walk the building to examine the facility, student work, posted materials
- Conversations with mentor principal, teachers, families and community members
- School improvement plan
- School mission statement
- Staff/faculty handbook
- Discipline code
- Master calendar and daily schedule
- Directives from district or CMO

- District evaluation of the school
- Discipline data *(including suspension and expulsion data)*
- Interim Results
- State Test Results
- Stakeholder satisfaction data generated by surveys, focus groups and informal discussions
- Teacher evaluations or personal professional development plans
- Curriculum materials (scope and sequence)

- Staff and teacher job descriptions
- Staff and teacher hiring process materials
- Professional development agendas
- Leadership team/ grade level/ department meeting agendas
- Newsletters
- Celebrations and rituals

Notes:

NOTICINGS/ POSSIBLE FOCUS AREAS:

QUICK SCHOOL ASSESSMENT GUIDE

Quick Data Analysis

Identify current student achievement levels to visualize the path to higher achievement levels for each student.

Project the growth needed for each of the first 3-5 years of your principalship to have 90% of your students at or above proficiency in Math and ELA.

Set a One Year proficiency target for ELA and for Math. Record it here:

Year 1 ELA proficiency target

QUICK SCHOOL ASSESSMENT GUIDE

Year 1 Math proficiency target

Add additional proficiency targets here:

Add details regarding data here:

SAMPLE OPEN HOUSE LETTER

DATE

Greetings Parents/Guardians

SCHOOL NAME will be holding its annual open house on DATE from TIME TO TIME. We are asking all parents and guardians to first meet in the school cafeteria at TIME for a brief introductory program.

During open house, teachers will have samples of student work available and an overview of the classroom expectations will be provided. Time will not permit us to discuss each child's performance in detail. If you wish, you will have the opportunity to schedule a more private, detailed conference.

By attending open house, your son/daughter will have the opportunity to earn additional Wildcat bucks, which can be used for prizes at school!

We value your presence and support. Together, we can assure that your child will have a successful year. See you at open house!

Sincerely,
Name
Principal

SAMPLE WELCOME LETTER/TEACHERS

Greetings, SCHOOL NAME Faculty and Staff:

My name is NAME, and I would like to take this opportunity to introduce myself as the Principal of SCHOOL NAME. I am very excited to begin this wonderful school year with you, full of wonderful changes! The theme for the year is: THEME. My educational belief is that all children deserve a quality education and that all children can achieve at high levels. At SCHOOL NAME we value:

Respect, Leadership, and Scholarship

My vision for the school is: To improve the educational opportunities, preparation, and academic results for all children at SCHOOL NAME. Our goal is to provide our scholars with the best education in a safe learning environment. At SCHOOL NAME, scholars will participate in a comprehensive curriculum, which emphasizes reading, writing and problem-solving, and they will have an early exposure to leadership skills that will increase their college and career readiness.

I am excited to have the opportunity to positively change the life path for children at SCHOOL NAME. I'm even more excited to be making this huge change with you as a valuable member of the team. The administrative team has spent countless hours and energy selecting the right "Change Agents" for our school. Congratulations! for being a member of what is going to be the best team in SCHOOL DISTRICT NAME. To kick off the school year, our THEME EVENT DATE TIME AND LOCATION Breakfast will begin promptly at 8 am. Professional dress is required (the following is not permitted: jeans, sneakers, flip-flops, shorts). Please bring a change of clothes to work in classrooms once on campus. Pre-planning week activities will be distributed during this time.

SAMPLE WELCOME LETTER/TEACHERS

IMPORTANT REMINDERS:

Classroom Setup: During the week of pre-planning, teachers will be given limited time to work in their classrooms. The building will be opened until 5 pm daily for those "worker bees" wishing to stay later to set up their classrooms.

Student Orientation: DATE AND TIME Parents will be allowed to visit the campus and do a quick meet and greet to help familiarize themselves with the campus. More information to come.

Enjoy the last few days of summer vacation, and I look forward to seeing you on DATE OF TEACHER RETURN!

Name
Title

SAMPLE MEETING CHECKLIST

Content Meeting Guide

TOPICS OF DISCUSSION	CHECK IF COVERED

1. Review of Lesson from Previous Week (including Pros & Cons)

NOTES:

2. Analysis of Student Work

A. Did each person bring a piece of student work?

NOTES:

3. Content Modifications (Did the team discuss any modifications they would make in the future? What scaffolding lesson needs to be taught?)

NOTES:

SAMPLE MEETING CHECKLIST

4. Standards to be Addressed This Week (Did the team discuss the standards to be covered?) What is the scholar's readiness to master the standard? What does the work look like for the highest level of the standard?

NOTES:

5. Did you Discuss A Plan for the Upcoming Week?

Notes:

6. Was there A Discussion of the Writing Strategies for the Upcoming Week?

NOTES:

7. Will you need Administrative Assistance?

Notes:

SAMPLE MINI HANDBOOK OUTLINE

SCHOOL NAME

THEME LOGO

School Wide Expectations Mini-Handbook 2018-2019

- Hallway Behavior:
  - Restroom Procedures
  - Cafeteria Procedures
  - Dismissal
- Classroom Safety Procedures:
  - Fire drill
  - Crisis/Code Red
- Discipline/Classroom Management:
  - In School Suspension
  - Dress Code
  - Technology
- Phones:
- Email:
- Attendance (Scholars):
  - Teacher and Paraprofessional Sign In/Sign Out
- Teacher and Staff Absence:
- Teacher and Staff Duty:
- Parent Teacher Conferences and Classroom Visits:
- Parent Communication:
- Data Notebooks:
- Mentor Teacher Program and New to SCHOOL NAME Teachers:
  - Faculty Meetings

SAMPLE OPENING DAY OF SCHOOL GUIDE

**Administrative Checklist
Opening Day of School**

☐ Check walkie talkies one week prior to school starting

☐ Check pa system two weeks prior to school starting

☐ Determine Arrival Time of Admin/Leadership Team:
　　TIME:

☐ Arrival Time of Teachers/Staff:
　　TIME

☐ Assign Duty Locations and Directions

SAMPLE OPENING DAY OF SCHOOL GUIDE

Sample Duty Directions

BUS DUTY:

- Elementary
  - Labels needed for students to have bus numbers on them (Print copies of bus numbers on labels) for bus duty.
- Secondary
  - Have bus rosters printed to capture student bus numbers.
- Car Rider
  - Elementary/Middle
- Color Codes/ Tags for car riders, Duty Staff determine if child will be a car rider at the end of the day.
- Teachers will create "How I will get home" Sheet for homeroom.
- Taking Attendance
  - TIME Due to the office
  - Manual Headcount NAME ASSIGNED TO
- Announcements
  - TIME Begin Morning Announcements.
  - Principal, STUDENTS NEED TO HEAR YOUR VOICE
- Campus Walk
  - TIME Campus Walk PRINCIPAL AND ADMIN Look for: overcrowded classrooms, instructional practices, teacher support needed, students who need support. District check-in.
- Lunch Walks
  - Create schedule for lunch room checks. Look for: overcrowded lunch times, efficiency of cafeteria staff, possible adjustments in schedule, opportunities for revised rules and expectations.

Sample Duty Directions [Continued]

- Dismissal
  - Dismissal Procedures: Start Time, Duty Locations Documents for parents?
- End of the Day send off!
  - Staff meets to quickly review the day and receive a treat.
  - As a result of the first day, draft 1st Day Review and email to celebrate what went well and address any mishaps or changes to procedures.
- REST REST REST REST!!!

Chapter 11:
HER STORY

CASE STUDY #1: JENNIFER BROWN

TELL ABOUT YOUR START IN EDUCATION.

Until the summer before my senior year in high school, I wanted to be a lawyer. My parents arranged for me to have a summer job working for a friend of the family who was an attorney, and I hated it! When I went off to college, I majored in English because I love literature so much. I actually entered the teaching profession through an alternate certification program that was quite rigorous. In hindsight, I think it prepared me very well, pedagogically. What's interesting is that my first teaching job was as an English teacher at a high school. I started on Valentine's Day by replacing a teacher who'd left mid-year. I wasn't much older than the juniors I taught, but I ended up loving the students. Since I entered the profession in a non-traditional way, I've continued to hold positions that are also non-traditional.

WHO DREW YOU TO BECOME AN ADMINISTRATOR?

I've never been a principal, and for a long time, I've had no desire to be one. I hold the position of principal in such high esteem. I've been fortunate to observe some amazing people who were really great leaders of schools. My favorite principal, Ron Thompson, was a retiree who decided he wasn't quite finished working, and he came to the middle school where I was working to help turn it around. He was unapologetic about providing low-income students access to Honors level courses, and because he upset the status quo in our school, he caught plenty of flak for it. I still admire the courage he displayed in making controversial leadership decisions that were in the best interest of children.

AS A FEMALE LEADER, WHAT HAS BEEN YOUR GREATEST CHALLENGE?

It's interesting that I'm struggling to answer this question. When I reflect on my journey to Executive Director, the challenges I've faced haven't necessarily been exclusive to women leaders. I've had a number of men advocate for me and promote me, but I've never felt that a position was inaccessible to me because of my gender. Perhaps, I'm a little cocky! ☺

KATRINA RILEY

AS A FEMALE LEADER, WHAT HAS BEEN THE MOST REWARDING EXPERIENCE?

Being in a position to mentor others and create opportunities for others have been most rewarding.

HOW HAVE YOU DEVELOPED OTHER FEMALE LEADERS?

I've always offered myself to be a mentor to women leaders, because mentors have been so integral to my development as a leader. I've also been a sponsor to aspiring leaders, and sponsorship is different from leadership. Sponsorship requires one to be in a key position to advocate for and hire another person. Now that I'm in my current role where I'm blessed to lead a network of schools, I have the opportunity to ensure that women are in key positions in my organization. This requires relationship building and providing feedback around their strengths and growth areas so that they're well-equipped to move to the next level when the opportunity arises.

WHAT CHARACTERISTICS DO YOU BELIEVE MAKE FEMALE LEADERS A KEY PART OF THE EDUCATIONAL PROCESS?

We tend to be coalition builders, which I think is very important. I think women leaders more readily embrace the notion that they cannot accomplish the mission alone. We, intentionally, build community by bringing others along.

WHAT DO YOU BELIEVE THE FUTURE OF EDUCATION LOOKS LIKE FOR FEMALE ADMINISTRATORS?

I think there will be more opportunities for entrepreneurship and leadership in the future. I see a world where more women create and lead charter, management organizations, and more women are appointed superintendents of major school districts around the country.

WHAT IS YOUR EDUCATIONAL PHILOSOPHY?

Interestingly enough, I think my philosophy has changed over time. In my current space, I wholeheartedly believe that Black children from low-income families can achieve at high academic levels, if given access to quality instruction and social-emotional supports. Lately, I find myself being quite vocal and unapologetic about my focus on Black children, because I feel it's MY calling. There are enough people who are concerned about other children; therefore, I choose to devote my life's work to Black students.

WHAT IS YOUR FAVORITE QUOTE THAT INSPIRES YOU AND YOUR EDUCATIONAL WORK?

It's actually a Bible verse: Luke 12:48 "To whom much is given, much is required."

KATRINA RILEY

WHAT ADVICE WOULD YOU GIVE TO NEW FEMALE LEADERS IN EDUCATION?

Another quote: "The first responsibility of a leader is to define the current reality." Max Depree. It's impossible to improve or propel whatever you're leading if you haven't accurately assessed the current state of affairs by collecting data from various parts of the organization. Implement and always practice sound decision- making skills.

Chapter 12:
HER STORY

CASE STUDY #2 IRANETTA WRIGHT

TELL ABOUT YOUR START IN EDUCATION.

As a little girl, I always knew I wanted to be a teacher. I loved teaching my sister and the other neighbors in the neighborhood. I was a Sunday school teacher at the age of twelve, and from that experience, I knew education was for me. When I went to college, I decided that I wasn't going to be a teacher because teachers did not make enough money. I went into what I thought would be pre-law and took my first international business class, and I hated it. I had a conversation with my grandfather, and he said, "follow your heart, and as long as you do what you love, you'll never work a day in your life." That was the beginning of my career in education, and shortly thereafter, I changed my major and earned a degree in special education.

WHO INSPIRED YOU TO BECOME AN ADMINISTRATOR?

I was on a sorority trip when I was a senior in college, and I saw these two elderly sorors. They were beautifully dressed, and I admired them from a distance. I had an opportunity to speak with them before we left the convention. In talking with them, I learned that they were educators. One of them was a Guidance Counselor; I don't recall the position the other soror held. We began talking about the field of education, and I shared my feelings regarding the low teacher salaries and how the low pay would impact me for the duration of my career. The two ladies filled me in on the fact that there was money in education and that many leaders in administration were able to make very lucrative salaries. The two women shared that they had observed leadership traits in me during the conference. They thought that I was a natural leader and that I'd be in leadership in no time. This was my senior year, and after graduating, I started my career in education as a teacher. I received my Master's degree in Educational Leadership and eventually went into administration.

WHAT HAS BEEN YOUR GREATEST CHALLENGE AS A FEMALE LEADER?

I am a focused kind of leader. I learned early on that if I were a male leader I would be considered strong and assertive; however, as a female leader, I was sometimes seen and perceived differently. Female leaders face the challenge of being seen as unempathetic, uncaring, and sometimes we can be seen as being a "bit" of a tyrant. I have been referenced by the use of the "B" word, which I choose not to use because it's hurtful. Furthermore, it could not be further from who I truly am. My focus is about children. I believe that education is serious, and it's a serious matter. It is our responsibility to make certain that we change the educational experiences for our children. Sometimes, we are the most stable person in the lives of some of our students. I don't want you to make the assumption that all children have instability in their lives, but many of the children that I've had the opportunity to serve have had instability in their life. As leaders in schools, it is our responsibility to be the objective voice for them and to treat every situation like we would if our own children were involved.

WHAT HAS BEEN THE MOST REWARDING AS A FEMALE LEADER?

I am a mentor at heart. As a former Assistant Superintendent and presently as a Deputy Superintendent, I really see being a mentor as a part of my responsibility. The most rewarding experience for me is recognizing the moment when the light bulb goes on. The "light bulb" going on experience symbolizes understanding and grasping. As a teacher, it was very rewarding when my students comprehended a concept. As a principal, it was rewarding for me when my teachers finally grasped a principle. I have supported administrators when they have gotten "it" and found success in a situation. Sometimes, you don't realize the impact that you have on others, until you have the opportunity to watch them step out *and do it* on their own. As a Deputy Superintendent, I have found satisfaction in hearing others repeat the wisdom I have shared with them or accepting the recommendations that I had made to them. Seeing those that I have mentored, as they train others, epitomizes the power in mentorship. I am joyful to know that there is something that I have done that is going to have a lasting impression on children for years to come. I was a great teacher, but I believe that my impact and my reach can be greater by touching more of those that were touching students. When I made the decision to leave the classroom and move into administration, I believed that my reach and my touch for children could be exponential.

HOW HAVE YOU DEVELOPED OTHER FEMALE LEADERS?

I have never been afraid to be honest with people, nor have I been afraid to give people credit for what they do. I recall my very first job as a principal; I had a vice principal at that time, and this was her first vice principal's job. Early on, she and I had a conversation, and she shared that she was nervous about working with a female leader. In the past, she had worked with female leaders who had created a competitive spirit between them. Immediately, this same individual realized that I was a different female leader who didn't have a desire to compete with her. Under my leadership, my desire is to model professionalism, promote a spirit of togetherness and implement the best practices to enable children to reach their potential. I work well with males and females, and I think female leaders recognize that I work well with them because I'm confident with who I am as a leader. Because I'm confident in myself, I don't have a challenge with not being the smartest one in the room, nor am I envious if someone else receives the honor and recognition for something they have accomplished. In addition, it is not a challenge for me to redirect, coach or mentor.

WHAT CHARACTERISTICS DO YOU BELIEVE MAKE FEMALE LEADERS A KEY PART OF THE EDUCATIONAL PROCESS?

Female leaders are resilient. Often females are the foundation of the family, having to be all things to so many; a wife, or mother a sister, a daughter and at the same time a leader. We wear so many hats and cannot afford not to do all these things well. Female leaders carry an extreme strength and an extreme challenge at the same time because if we don't keep all of the things in order, then we are no good to anybody and so we have to make sure that we are maintaining a balance. It is important to acknowledge that everybody's balance is different, so what may be a plate too full for one person may not be a plate too full for someone else. I learned early on in my career that my plate was larger than most, and I could carry and take a lot on my plate but I was really good about making sure that I knew when my plate was full and I wouldn't accept anything else.

WHAT DO YOU BELIEVE THE FUTURE OF EDUCATION LOOKS LIKE FOR FEMALE ADMINISTRATORS?

I think without female administrators there is no future for education. An area of growth for female leaders is the area of superintendency. While female leaders make up a large portion of the teacher force and the principal force that number is not as large when it comes to those in superintendent positions.

WHAT IS YOUR EDUCATIONAL PHILOSOPHY?

I believe that all children, regardless of their race, their gender, their ethnicity or socioeconomic status, deserve a high quality education. As leaders, It is our responsibility to make certain that we are giving them the absolute best, or we're going to die trying.

WHAT IS YOUR FAVORITE QUOTE THAT INSPIRES YOU AND YOUR EDUCATIONAL WORK?

"Every decision I make has a child's face on it." As a novice administrator, I actually heard this quote from a mentor. If we are just randomly making decisions, we lose the importance of making child-centric decisions, and true authentic growth and transformation will not happen when we lose sight of what's necessary for children.

WHAT ADVICE WOULD YOU GIVE TO NEW FEMALE LEADERS IN EDUCATION?

To thine own self be true. Don't be afraid to take risks; don't be afraid to ask questions; don't be afraid to surround yourself with people that are positive; and don't be afraid to be around people who are perceived to know more than you. Recognize that there is a balance, but don't let anyone dictate what that balance is. Have someone in your life who loves you in spite of. This will help you when you're doing the tough work for children. Realize that it will not always be popular, and you will not always be popular. there will be nights when you will lie in bed, and you will cry in your pillow because of the things that will have been said to you, about you, or around you. When this happens, recall the quote that says "every decision that I make has a child's face on it." Live this work such that when you go to sleep you are comfortable with the decisions made that day. Sometimes, you might not make the right decision, but be assured that the decision you made was for the right reason. Lastly, know that mistakes are not fatal or final. Learn and grow from them!

Chapter 13:

HER STORY

CASE STUDY #3 SONIA MARTIN

TELL ABOUT YOUR START IN EDUCATION.

*L*IFE AS A student was very challenging for me. The mold for "one size fits all" teaching and learning was broken when I enrolled as a kindergarten student at Adolph Meyer Elementary School. My ability to fully acquire the essential skills and concepts needed to comprehend subject area content was limited. Throughout my K-12 educational career, I felt a sense of shame and humiliation because my peers were excelling, and I was barely getting by with my coursework. The picture I painted for myself did not include a path to higher learning. It was not until my mother said to me with determination in her voice, "You will go to college." In that moment, I felt a huge sense of accountability to her, and I was overwhelmed at the thought of not accomplishing the goal. Immediately, after my high school graduation, I enrolled in Southern University at New Orleans and majored in Elementary Education. However, my passion for teaching did not develop until my junior year of college. It was after I had developed a sense of self-efficacy to create a difference in my own ability to learn that my passion grew. I no longer had to contend with the impression that I was incapable of learning. From this point on, I was committed to helping children learn by any means necessary.

WHO INSPIRED YOU TO BECOME AN ADMINISTRATOR?

My peers led me to believe that I embodied the qualities of a leader, and they encouraged me to pursue an Educational Leadership degree. I was unaware of my skill set as a leader. Every initiative and/or learning experience that I engaged in was done out of a natural response to create optimal educational opportunities for all students.

WHAT HAS BEEN YOUR GREATEST CHALLENGE AS A FEMALE LEADER?

One of my greatest leadership challenges was enlisting others in the process for change. During my wonder years as a school administrator, I didn't quite understand why it was difficult for some people to change. As I grew as a leader, I have learned that change is difficult. In education, change is inevitable to create thriving learning communities. Therefore, I approach every growth opportunity intended for those I lead and myself with relentless pursuit and fierce resolve, in my heart, to accomplish a collective goal. I go with those who are ready for change, and I am present for those who need to catch up.

WHAT HAS BEEN THE MOST REWARDING AS A FEMALE LEADER?

It makes my heart happy when I see challenging students begin to positively respond to the quality time I have invested in getting to know all about them, including their personal interests, academic goals and aspirations. I believe in the power of positive relationships and the influence it can have on students' behavioral outcomes.

HOW HAVE YOU DEVELOPED OTHER FEMALES?

I have developed females by providing them with a system of support that involves open communication and coaching through meaningful relationships that are inspiring, encouraging, relevant and reliable with associated content knowledge and availability.

WHAT ARE THE CHARACTERISTICS THAT MAKE FEMALE LEADERS A KEY PART OF THE EDUCATIONAL PROCESS?

The key to success in education is having a growth mindset, expert knowledge in the field, passion for teaching and learning, compassion, initiative, open communication, visible presence, mental toughness, problem solving skills, flexibility, winning attitude, and unconditional love.

WHAT ARE YOUR BELIEFS ON THE FUTURE OF EDUCATION FOR FEMALE ADMINISTRATORS?

Doors are opening for females to lead and prosper schools and districts. As long as female leaders believe in their ability to lead and make a difference, they will be successful.

WHAT IS YOUR EDUCATIONAL PHILOSOPHY?

All children can learn, when learning is facilitated with the right combination of researched based instructional practices and resources.

WHAT IS YOUR FAVORITE QUOTE?

People are often unreasonable, irrational, and self-centered. Forgive them anyway.
If you are kind, people may accuse you of being selfish and having ulterior motives. Be kind anyway.
If you are successful, you will win some unfaithful friends and some genuine enemies. Succeed anyway.

If you are honest and sincere, people may deceive you.
   Be honest and sincere anyway.
What you spend years creating, others could destroy overnight. Create anyway.
If you find serenity and happiness, some may be jealous. Be happy anyway.
The good you do today will often be forgotten. Do good anyway.
Give the best you have, and it will never be enough. Give your best anyway.
In the final analysis, it is between you and God. It was never between you and them anyway.

-Mother Teresa

WHAT ADVICE WOULD YOU GIVE TO NEW FEMALE LEADERS IN EDUCATION?

The best advice that I can give to new females in leadership is "Know your worth and potential."

Chapter 14:
HER STORY

CASE STUDY #4: KRYSTAL LOFTON

TELL ABOUT YOUR START IN EDUCATION.

THE OFFICIAL START to my education began, at an early age, while listening and watching my grandmother and mother teach students at church and school. My family has been big advocates of education, especially my grandparents, given the fact that they were raised to believe that educations was the key to success. This sense of valuing education was instilled in me as early as I can remember.

My mother is a retired music teacher, and I remember always being by her side watching her instruct students. It was a magical experience to watch her teach students how to read music and create beautiful sounds by using their voice or instruments.

I started my career as a 1st grade teacher in 1992 after graduating from the great Florida A&M University. I worked as a first-grade teacher for 7 years. During that time, I completed a Master's

Degree in Educational Leadership. After working for 7 years as a 1st grade teacher, I transferred to a school closer to my home and taught 2nd grade. Within that year, I also applied to be a part of the first cadre of reading coaches in our district and was accepted into the program. After 1 year of working as a reading coach, I was appointed Assistant Principal, and after 3 years of working as an AP, I was appointed Principal in our district. This is my 26th year working in our district and year 14 as a school administrator. I will attach my resume' for your viewing.

WHO MADE YOU WANT TO BECOME AN ADMINISTRATOR?

I grew up in a home of educators. My grandmother, grandfather and mother were educators. After rebuilding my relationship with my biological father later in my life, I found out that my grandfather on my father's side was the first black Principal to open the all black school for high school students in Plant City, Florida.

I was actually drawn to become an administrator because I saw so many decisions being made for our students of color that were unfair and unjustified. Particularly, our young, black boys were being labeled and placed in Exceptional Student Education programs and viewed as unreachable or unmotivated to learn. It became my desire to move in a position where I could lead discussions around cultural differences and biases, as well as "break" the academic struggles that our students face today.

KATRINA RILEY

WHAT HAS BEEN YOUR GREATEST CHALLENGE AS A FEMALE LEADER?

One of the greatest challenges I face as a female leader is being given the same opportunities as our male counterparts. I see many male leaders moving up in the educational systems as Directors, Area Superintendents and Supervisors. Yet, their track record of success does not support the new appointments in the position. I find that I have to continuously prove myself by demonstrating a knowledge of the curriculum, while building school capacity and creating school conditions that encourage positive relationships.

WHAT HAS BEEN MOST REWARDING TO YOU AS A FEMALE LEADER?

The most rewarding events in my work have always been empowering others to move forward, especially female educators. I enjoy empowering teachers to embrace a growth mindset versus a fixed mindset in order to change the course of their destiny. One of my favorite quotes that I have painted on my office wall states "Today, I have the power to change my story." This quote is a powerful message to encourage my teachers to dig deep, believe in themselves and watch God work. Because I have a very close relationship with God, I will often refer to God's favor, grace and mercy which sometimes leads to an all out bible study session in my office. ☺ When I became a Principal many years ago, I asked God to give me eyes to see, ears to hear and a spirit of discernment to help guide my path as I lead others. To me, it is so important to make sure I am sending the right message to my students, staff, parents and the community about what I stand for, and I will always work to do what is best for students.

HOW HAVE YOU DEVELOPED OTHER FEMALE LEADERS?

I have helped develop female leaders by making sure they are always informed and put in front about upcoming leadership opportunities. In most cases, I will tell my female teachers that I have signed them up for leadership opportunities within the school, such as School Advisory Council chair, Instructional Leadership Team chair, Team Facilitators and opportunities to sit on the leadership team. I send my female teacher to district trainings, and upon their return to the school site, I schedule opportunities for them to present information to the faculty and staff. On many occasions, I will send female teachers to state trainings as well, because I am a believer in networking and building your experiences.

WHAT ARE THE CHARACTERISTICS THAT MAKE FEMALE LEADERS A KEY PART OF THE EDUCATIONAL PROCESS?

Female leaders are key in the educational process because they lead with compassion and sensitivity to the needs of all students. They have an appreciative lens that reflect the goals and aspirations of their students and what is required for success building for the future.

KATRINA RILEY

WHAT DOES THE FUTURE OF EDUCATION LOOK LIKE FOR FEMALE ADMINISTRATORS?

As I see the number of female Superintendents being appointed across the nation as well as in upper district level positions, I am hopeful that this will not be the new trend but the norm. We must make opportunities happen, if they are not being created for us. As female administrators, we must work harder to be recognized for the great work that is happening at our schools and within our districts. It is important for us to put our work out front and celebrate our small wins. Build capacity by creating appreciative and lasting relationships within your organization. Work with community partners to build stronger relationships between school and home, and be your own best motivator by marketing your work for others to see.

WHAT IS YOUR EDUCATIONAL PHILOSOPHY?

All students can learn…no matter what. Education can be full of challenges, yet rewarding with excitement and joy. As a Principal, I believe in creating conditions that support diverse experiences in education, performance management and system change. It is my goal to provide opportunities and empowerment while maintaining high levels of professionalism.

WHEN SHE LEADS

WHAT IS YOUR FAVORITE QUOTE THAT INSPIRES YOU AND YOUR EDUCATIONAL WORK?

My favorite quote/poem is from Marianne Williamson's book—A Return to Love titled Our Deepest Fear.

*Our deepest fear is not that we are inadequate
fear is that we are powerful beyond measure.*

It is our light, not our darkness that frightens us.

*We ask ourselves
Who am I to be brilliant, gorgeous, talented, fabulous?
Actually, who are you not to be?
You are a child of God.*

*Your playing small
Does not serve the world.
There's nothing enlightening about shrinking
So that other people won't feel insecure around you.*

*We are all meant to shine,
As children do.
We were born to make manifest
The glory of God that is within u.*

*It's not just in some of us;
It's in everyone.*

And as we let our own light shine,
We unconsciously give other people permission to do the same.
As we're liberated from our own fear,
Our presence automatically liberates others.

I know it's not a small quote, but it's my favorite. ☺

WHAT ADVICE WOULD YOU GIVE TO NEW FEMALE LEADERS IN EDUCATION?

Be strategic in everything you do. Think big and know that fear is not an option. Stand and be great!

Chapter 15:

HER STORY

CASE STUDY #5 DEBORAH WARD

TELL US ABOUT YOUR START IN EDUCATION.

Growing up in West Virginia and returning home after graduation, did not provide or offer very many teaching job opportunities for a female of color. Fortunately or unfortunately, I had a death in my family in Cleveland, Ohio. After traveling to the service and meeting some relatives for the first time, I was encouraged to return to seek an educational job. Having grown up in a small coal mining town in the mountains of West Virginia, I was afraid to assume or even apply for a high school teaching position in the city of Cleveland. I was uncertain of my skills in handling the demands of an urban school teaching position; therefore, I took a position with a neighboring Ohio police department as a dispatcher. After several months into the school year, I was encouraged, by a friend, to apply for a teaching position. I was offered a high school teaching position and remained in the position for 11 years. This was the beginning of my start in education.

WHO INSPIRED YOU TO BECOME AN ADMINISTRATOR?

I became an administrator due to the retirement of a current administrator who recommended me to assume her position. I did not feel ready and did not want the position. The Board of Education asked me to hold the position for two weeks until they found someone and two weeks led to several years.

WHAT HAS BEEN YOUR GREATEST CHALLENGE AS A FEMALE LEADER?

My greatest challenge as a female leader has been the ability to balance being both female and African American. I have experienced inequity and racism in the hiring process as well as a salary inequity.

WHAT HAS BEEN THE MOST REWARDING EXPERIENCE AS A FEMALE LEADER?

The most rewarding part of being a female leader is to be a role model for other females who have aspirations of leadership.

KATRINA RILEY

HOW HAVE YOU DEVELOPED OTHER FEMALE LEADERS?

I have served as a leadership coach and mentor for many female leaders.

WHAT CHARACTERISTICS DO YOU BELIEVE MAKE FEMALE LEADERS A KEY PART OF THE EDUCATIONAL PROCESS?

Characteristics I believe that make female leaders a key part of the educational process are compassion, self-awareness, listening skills, and empathy.

WHAT DO YOU BELIEVE THE FUTURE OF EDUCATION LOOKS LIKE FOR FEMALE ADMINISTRATORS?

I believe the future for female administrators is very bright. There will always be opportunities for females who have the desire and the passion to lead.

WHAT IS YOUR EDUCATIONAL PHILOSOPHY?

My educational philosophy is to make every decision based on what is best for children. This philosophy should be implemented, regardless of your leadership position.

WHEN SHE LEADS

WHAT IS YOUR FAVORITE QUOTE THAT INSPIRES YOU AND YOUR EDUCATIONAL WORK?

I've learned that people will forget what you said; people will forget what you did, but people will never forget how you made them feel.

Maya Angelou

WHAT ADVICE WOULD YOU GIVE TO NEW FEMALE LEADERS IN EDUCATION?

My advice would be to always acquire a mentor. Find someone who has been a successful leader and allow yourself to be vulnerable to both positive and negative feedback.

A CALL TO ACTION

As a new principal, my experiences were so vast. There was so much information coming from so many places, and the momentum was ongoing. In an attempt to keep the pace, I often found myself scrambling for information. It has been my greatest mission to create ways to empower and support other aspiring and current educational leaders in ways that I wish I had been afforded. #Principalnerd became a movement purposed to grow great leaders. #Principalnerd supports school leaders with the #Principalnerd

Assistant Principal Academy, quarterly newsletter, training webinars, and individual/team leadership coaching. Join the movement, as we convince annually for the the When She Leads: School Leadership conferences and leadership lunch and learns.

ABOUT THE AUTHOR

With over twenty years of service as an educational leader, Katrina Riley is a phenomenal educator who has served in many roles with a mission to cultivate new generations of industry leaders to better serve children. Katrina has worked in multiple educational settings in various locations including: Louisiana, Massachusetts, Maryland, and Florida, her home state.

She has served in multiple roles, including teacher, coach, principal and mentor. Katrina holds a Bachelor's degree in English from Florida State University and a Master's degree in Educational Leadership from Nova Southeastern University. In 2010, Katrina completed the New Leaders for New Schools Principal Residency Program in New Orleans, Louisiana. She has extensive experience in a myriad of educational settings, including public, charter, nonprofit, school-based and district levels. Her most recent work has been as an urban school principal where she was instrumental in transforming schools and communities. In 2016, Katrina attended the National Institute for Urban School Leaders at the

Principal's Center at Harvard University. During her time as a principal, Katrina implemented inaugural school wide programs in partnership with AmeriCorps. As a mentor, she has assisted other educators by providing support in helping them to positively impact children. Katrina has been active in various community and civic organizations, including being a participant in the Focus on Leadership Development Cohort in Gainesville, Fl, a member of The Urban League- Young Professionals and an active member of Delta Sigma Theta Sorority, Incorporated. Katrina can be described as an innovator and motivator who founded #Principalnerd, an online resource for school leaders.

As the author of When She Leads, Katrina hopes to energize new audiences and to continuously empower and inspire school leaders. Katrina currently resides in Orange Park, Florida.

Connect with KATRINA RILEY on Social Media

- **f** PRINCIPALNERDTRIBE
- **@** @PRINCIPALNERD
- **in** KATRINA-RILEY-68105B138
- **🐦** @PRINCIPALNERD1

www.ingramcontent.com/pod-product-compliance
Lightning Source LLC
Chambersburg PA
CBHW052025070526
44584CB00016B/1906